UNCOMMON SENSE
The Flip Side of Conventional Thinking

UNCOMMON SENSE
The Flip Side of Conventional Thinking

By Bharat Bhatia and Gaurav Bhatia

Edited by Gaurav Bhatia and Xing Hang

Uncommon Sense: The Flip Side of Conventional Thinking/ by Bharat Bhatia and Gaurav Bhatia

ISBN 978-0-578-00799-1

About the Authors

Uncommon Sense is a collaborative project between the team of twin brothers Bharat and Gaurav Bhatia. They each have their own talents and interests that contributed to this book. Bharat got his bachelor's degree in therapeutic recreation from the University of Georgia in 2005. He also got certified as a personal trainer through the American Council on Exercise. In 2006, Bharat left personal training to join the family jewelry business and still works there.

Gaurav got his bachelor's degree in public relations at Georgia State University. He is currently works at Georgia State University as an activities coordinator and is also doing a master's program in education. Gaurav's main job at Georgia State is working with an organization called After School All-stars, which provides after school activities for underprivileged middle schools.

Both of the Bhatia brothers are actively involved in community service. They have been involved with Red Cross, Habitat for Humanity, March of Dimes, and many other organizations. Bharat spent some time volunteering at a refugee center called International Rescue Committee (IRC), and now he collects computer and other donations for the IRC.

Much of the content in this book relates to the experiences of the two brothers, but there are also many subjects that do not directly relate to their experience. Some ideas in this book are for information while other ideas are for entertainment. Either way, we hope you benefit from this book.

Table of contents

New Ideas For Government

More Diversity on Capitol Hill

One of the reasons that government practices a faulty model is because it is run almost entirely by lawyers. Lawyers deal with court cases that are usually based on winners and losers, guilty and innocent, prosecutor and defendants, etc. There is very little cooperation in law. Having more business people would help, but we also need other people to keep businesses from abusing their power. After all, look what happened when Wall Street economists controlled the Federal Reserve and US Treasury; we got a bailout that favored giving hand-outs to big business (socialism for the rich?). Having scientists in politics would benefit education and the environment. While current politicians often cater to the oil industry and other businesses to get votes, scientists can get support from their own community to enact environmental policies. Having people who work in charitable organisations would help balance out policies so that they wouldn't just benefit a few super-wealthy people at the expense of the poor. Red Cross helped draft the Geneva Conventions, so they can play a good role in national government. Having a diverse range of people can help keep any one area from gaining too much power.

Of course, there is a reason that we don't have more diversity in the government. It's not that voters refuse to vote a president who is a scientist or Red Cross employee. Scientists and people involved in charitable organizations do not get involved in politics, which is why they do not get elected. I think the solution to this problem is that governments should partner with charities. For example, Red Cross contributed greatly to the Geneva Conventions. The Geneva Conventions are guidelines that the United Nations use for international law. I would like to see the Red Cross involved further in politics, particularly in national and local governments. In fact, I would also like to see other charitable organizations involved in government. People in these organizations do not need to run for political office, but politicians can work with them as they work with many businesses.

One concern that may arise if charitable organizations were involved in politics is that charitable organizations would become corrupt after getting involved in politics. An argument against this concern is that nonprofit organizations have already been involved in politics and have made great contributions to society as a result of this. For instance, after the Red Cross was involved in the establishment of the Geneva Conventions, the global community has been more involved in providing medical care to wounded soldiers, as well as being involved in the extended protection of civilians, including relief workers, and prisoners of war during armed conflict. One of the biggest benefits that nonprofit organizations have contributed to politics is addressing civil rights. Groups like the American Civil Liberties Union have fought against racism, sexism, homophobia, and other forms of discrimination. Many victories have resulted from this, including the removal of state bans on interracial marriages, the legalization of same-sex marriages in California, and women gaining greater access to reproductive rights. Also, agencies such as International Rescue Committee and Refugee Family Services have gotten involved in politics by helping refugees receive the training they need to become citizens of America, including providing knowledge of U.S. laws and getting access to legalized employment. So the likelihood of charitable organizations becoming corrupt as a result of involvement in politics is very slim, as they are already involved and are making major improvements in society with little to no side effects.

Scientists would contribute greatly to government by improving support for alternative fuel sources. Although I believe the free market is better than government intervention, I feel that the US government subsidizes the oil industry way too much. As long as energy policy is influenced by government, it might as well be influenced in the right direction.

Government of the People

We often hear that America is a government of the people, for the people, and by the people. Although America is one of the most free countries in the world, it is still not a true democracy. Americans do not have any control over the laws. The only control we have is that we get to vote politicians in office. However, politicians make many promises, and we do not have any control over keeping them accountable. If they do a bad job, we have the option to vote for somebody else next time, but very few politicians truly serve the people. They usually just do enough to get elected or re-elected and often cater to special interest groups. In fact, even if there are a few politicians who truly care about the people, it is hard for them to get elected if they cannot market well, or if the party doesn't endorse them. This is especially true for the president. For example, Ron Paul and Rudolph Juliani ran for president. I would have voted for Ron Paul. I am sure that many Americans would vote for Rudolph Juliani because of his great leadership during the September 11 terrorist attacks as well as his sucessful job reducing crime in New York City. However, we did not have the choice because the Republican party nominated John McCain. This is the same for the Democratic primaries. The Democratic party chose Barack Obama, so Americans did not have a choice to vote for Hillary Clinton or any other Democratic candidate. So Americans do not vote for their leader but instead vote for whoever is left over after the parties weed out who they do not like. In fact, even after the nominees are chosen, the popular vote by Americans does not determine the president but rather than electoral college, which consists of the Senators, House of Representatives, and the Vice President in case of a tie. Although the electoral college usually picks the same candidate as the popular vote, there are exceptions. It seems odd that there should be any exceptions at all. Now don't get me wrong. I think America is a very free country, but it is free because the government allows me to live my life freely. In a way, the right to vote is irrelevant. What matters more is how your representatives treat you whether you voted for them or not.

While many Americans say that it is our patriotic duty to vote, I say that if our vote has very little voice, then it is really just a matter of personal choice whether to vote or not. Who you vote for does not always affect the outcome of the country. Generally, whoever we vote for will do very few of the things they promise. Patriotism is not just about voting and going to wars; it is also about taking action to improve your country. Community service, donating to charity, and raising money for charity are ways to serve your country.

Instead of full-time governors and members of Congress, government should be more like a board of directors. In Congress, most of their activity is just giving and listening to speeches. Very little is actually accomplished. This is a waste of taxpayer money. Government would be much more efficient if Congress and the president had other jobs. Congressional meetings would be once per week, and maybe twice per week during major issues. To keep from interfering with work, these meetings can be during the weekend. Maybe some can even be Friday at night. Any company that spends most of their time having board meetings would go out of businesses. Current governments only survive because they force people to pay taxes. If people in government had other jobs, they wouldn't need salaries, or they would at least have a smaller salary. This means more of taxpayer money would go towards developing the country rather than paying Congressional and presidential salaries.

Now what would happen to all those full-time Congress men and women? One idea is that they can go back to working in law firms. Most of them were lawyers before they entered politics. They can also try working any other job they want. They can start a business. There are many options.

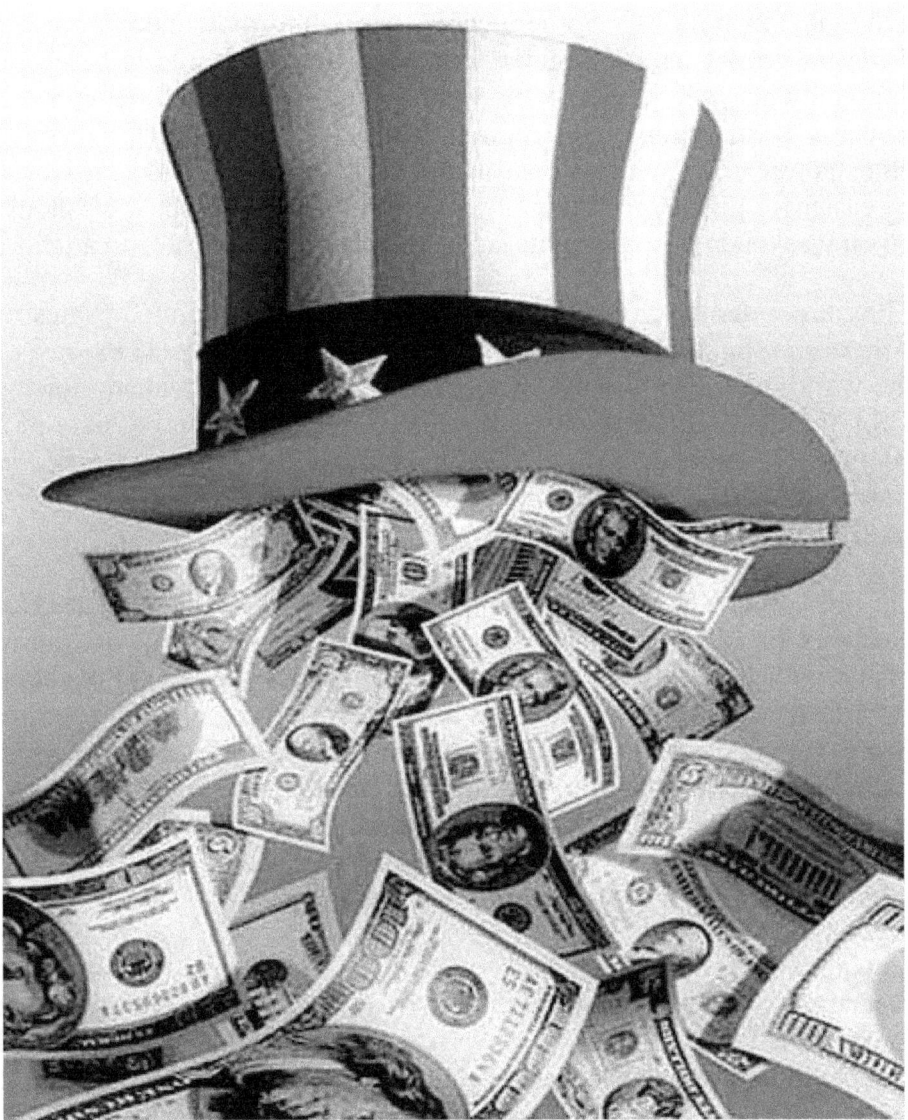

It would be a bad idea to immediately implement this policy. Maybe the government should gradually start having fewer Congressional meetings and lowering salary, but give members of Congress the opportunity to work other side jobs.

Maybe the reason why government is run mostly by lawyers is that people outside of law don't want to get involved in politics. If you have a successful business or a 9-5 job that you enjoy, why would you leave it for politics? Some people may, but most people won't. Lawyers do not have a regular schedule. Their schedule is based on appointments with clients who want to sue or who are being sued. Because lawyers have an irregular schedule, it is easier for them to enter politics. If Congressional meetings were less frequent, it would be easier for people outside of law to enter politics. Maybe they should be on weekends or weeknights so the average citizen is able to attend.

This direct democracy may not be practical for the United States of America at this time. In fact, because the US greatly affects the rest of the world, and also because of terrorism, it may be unrealistic for the USA to have a direct democracy ever. It might only be possible in a country less dependent on their military. Japan and many countries in Europe may be more able to experiment with
direct democracy.

On the other hand, America doesn't really need more powerful weapons to fight terrorism. America can already destroy the entire planet with its weapons; I am not advocating that we get rid of them. As long as we have a military that has access to these weapons, we are just as safe under a direct democracy as we are in our current situation. After all, America's military did not prevent the September 11 terrorist attacks, and this is despite having intelligence in which America already knew about the attack. America needs more military intelligence and not more powerful weapons.

Having the largest military in the world has not prevented terrorism. In fact, the US military, and even the CIA, have done many things that have fueled the anger of terrorists. The CIA has assassinated democratically elected leaders in other countries or rigged elections to remove them to put a leader that benefits America's business interests. The CIA put the Shah of Iran in power even though Iranians democratically elected somebody else. This was all just so America can get cheap oil. America invaded Iraq under the lies that Iraq had nuclear weapons and Iraq was involved in the September 11 terrorist attack.

In a direct democracy, without full-time Congress members, taxes would be lower because they would not be needed to pay for Congressional salaries. We could remove income taxes. Because meetings would be less frequent, this would save even more money. Maybe we can remove other taxes such as taxes on stocks and other gains. In fact, maybe we can even remove sales taxes. So how would government make enough money to support military, the fire departments, and law enforcement? Donations would be the best option, but another option is to have a monthly protection fee. Just as car insurance is required by law for drivers, this monthly fee could charged per household. We can also do a combination of donations and fees.

Some people may worry that Americans would not donate to a fire department or police force. This would not be a problem because millions of Americans already donate to charities such as the Fraternal Order of Police. After removing income tax, payroll taxes, taxes on stocks, and other unnecessary taxes; Americans would have more money, and they would be more willing to donate to the police, military, fire department, etc. In fact, if the military spent more time doing relief work and less on wars, this would also increase donations. The military currently does relief work in other countries; they just need to do more of it and spend less time in war. Relying on donations would allow Americans to have more control over the military and thus keep them accountable.

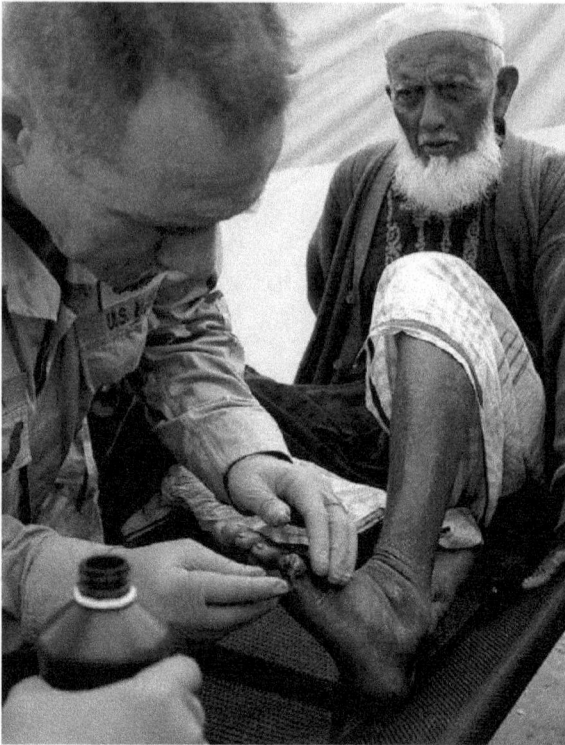

In fact, even Congress can rely on donations. Americans already donate to presidential campaigns and political parties. If Congress relied primarily on donations, they could easily raise enough money if they actually do a good job. Americans can donate more money if they feel the government is doing a good job, and they can donate less if they feel government is doing a bad job. This is a good way to keep Congress accountable.

Some people might worry that if Americans did not have to give taxes to the governments, then they would keep the money for themselves, and government would not function. Government can still collect taxes from toll booths, business licenses fees, duties on imports, and property taxes. Taxes and other government fees are fine as long as they involve actual services performed by the government. If Americans feel that the US government is doing a good job, they will have no problem donating money. There are millions of Americans who feel a sense of pride and patriotism; getting them to donate would not be difficult.

If direct democracy is impossible, maybe we can have a deliberative democracy, which is a combination of a direct democracy, and what we have now. Maybe we can keep our current government but allow the civilian population to have more control. Congress currently has a Senate and House of Representatives. Maybe Congress can also include a "Civilian Parliament" that consists of civilians who are able to vote on Congressional issues. Votes from these civlians would count just as much as votes from other members of Congress. The power of the civilian vs. Regular Congress would be based on numbers. This civilian government can be funded through donations.

This idea is not completely new. Switzerland actually incorporates direct democracy. Citizens can suggest ammendments to the constitution if they have 100,000 signatures within 18 months. In fact, citizens can overturn new laws of Parliament. The minimum requirement is having a petition with at least 50,000 votes within 100 days before passing the law. Although this is not easy, this is a far better example of freedom than we have in the US. To learn more about the Swiss government structure, check out the following link:

http://www.eda.admin.ch/eda/en/home/reps/ocea/vaus/infoch/chpoli.html

It is unlikely that the government will actually read what I am saying and actually implement these policies. However, we as Americans must do something to get more power in running the government. I guess the only way we can get closer to direct democracy is by getting involved in non-government organizations and doing government's work for them. For example, to gradually replace government welfare, we can support homeless shelters, Habitat for Humanity, the HandsOn Network, Red Cross, and other charities that work locally. To replace foreign aid, we can get more involved and donate to organizations like CARE, Red Cross, Computers for Africa, Grameen Bank, Water Aid, and many other organizations. Organizations such as CARE and Grameen Bank provide micro loans for the poor, which helps provide basic necessities to help poor people get out of the cycle of poverty. And then they repay these loans; they are able to afford it because the loans are managed well enough to help them start successful businesses. CARE also provides other economic aid by teaching farming techniques that produce more food and building schools to help educate people to become professionals.

Water Aid builds infrastructure for transferring water. For more information on these organizations, here are some of their websites:

CARE
http://www.care.org/index.asp?

HandsOn Network
http://www.handsonnetwork.org/

American Red Cross
http://www.redcross.org/

International Red Cross
http://www.icrc.org/ and http://www.ifrc.org/

Grameen Bank Foundation
http://www.grameenfoundation.org/

Computer For Africa
http://computers4africa.org/

Water Aid
http://www.wateraid.org/

World Toilet Organization
http://www.worldtoilet.org/

The work of these organizations has done far more good than any government welfare program, stimulus package, foreign aid, or military intervention. The World Bank's own statistics show that that as foreign aid increases, per capita income in sub-Saharan Africa generally decreases.

Military aid and foreign aid may solve some problems but create other ones in their place. Government welfare may keep somebody off of the streets, but it burdens taxpayers, and keeps welfare recipients from achieving anything. Non-government organizations (NGOS) often benefit the people without side effects. When did the work of CARE or Red Cross lead to terrorist attacks? I am sure terrorists have destroyed buildings of charity organizations, but they never became terrorists as a result of any action taken by these organizations. In fact, these organizations are probably helping prevent many children from becoming potential terrorists. Military intervention, on the other hand, often gives people a reason to become terrorists.

Now I cannot totally blame government for being involved in domestic welfare programs and foreign aid. Voters demand that politicians deal with issues. The economy is suffering, so voters want the president to put policies that help people who are poor or out of a job. Welfare programs, limitations on imports, and restrictions on outsourcing jobs are ways that a president may try to help people who are suffering economically. If the president simply says, "this isn't the government's job; it is best run by the private sector," then voters will not vote this person back into office. The same can be true for a president who does not deal with healthcare, foreign affairs, etc. So I suggest that instead of using tax money to create government programs to deal with these problems, the president should use his or her leadership position to promote non-government charities. Bill Clinton is still a politician, but he has a non-government charity organization called the William J. Clinton Foundation. The Clinton Foundation is involved in HIV prevention & treatment, economic development, healthcare, and many other causes. For more information about his organisation, go to http://www.clintonfoundation.org/.

Ralph Nader is also involved in non-governmental charity organizations dealing with the environment as well as consumer rights. Al Gore also promotes environmental welfare through non-governmental means. His website is http://www.algore.com/. Although I do not agree with Al Gore that global warming is a bigger threat than terrorism, I agree that pollution and environmental destruction are large problems that we need to deal with. I also agree with how he promotes his message through non-government means.

The current president and other politicians should follow a similar practice of these politicians. Instead of trying to use tax money to create government programs to change the system, politicians should use their position to collect voluntary donations to change the system. If politicans can raise private donations for their campaigns and political parties, they should have no problem raising money for charitable causes. Being the leader of the country does not require using tax money to tackle problems.

As much as I may criticize the government, overall, I think the US government does a good job. Well, the government does a good job by being less involved in our lives than most other governments. In most cases, I feel very free living in America. I can freely believe what I want, watch whatever movies I want, wear almost anything I want (i.e. cannot go naked or wear my underwear on the streets, but just about anything else is fair game), etc. If I criticise the president, nobody will arrest me. In some countries, you can get executed for criticizing the leader. So overall, I am lucky to be living in such a great country, but my country still can improve. A parent, friend, lover, or any other relationship will try to tell you when you are wrong even if most things you do are right. So you can argue that I am being patriotic to suggest how my country can be even better.

Bailing Out Americans After the Bailout

The government is spending over $700 billion to help out large companies such as AIG, Lehman Brothers, and Washington Mutual. I'm not a financial expert, but I think that when somebody has a ton of money and blows it, you don't give them more. People who blow money are the last people who you should trust with money. But according to the US government, that rule doesn't apply. The guys who we are bailing out are largely responsible for our economy collapsing, so I don't know why we are giving them more money. Okay, to be fair, it isn't just the Wall Street millionaires who are at fault. Millions of Americans took loans for houses that they couldn't afford. The banks are also at fault for giving those loans. So the American government is bailing out big banks and big Wall Street firms, but they won't bail out middle-class and lower-class Americans.

Since I can't stop the bailout, I would like to give the government some ideas on how not to waste tax dollars even further. Let me just give those guys in government basics. First of all, the national debt has reached $10 trillion and is still growing. And, you guys in the White House, do you know why that is? Go ahead, don't be afraid to answer. Confused? Okay, here it is. When you SPEND MORE money than you make, that INCREASES DEBT. So how do we reduce the debt? I know, that's a tricky question. Don't worry, you don't get penalized for guessing. Still having trouble coming up with an answer? Okay, here's the answer...YOU SPEND LESS. Oh my gosh...how do we do that? Well, I know this is a tough one, so let me give you a crash course.

The first thing to do is remove unnecessary expenses. You've probably been told that that the war in Iraq is costing you hundreds of billions of dollars. Well, I won't drill that on you again and again, so here are some other ideas.

It wouldn't hurt if you guys withdrew military bases from countries like Saudi Arabia. That would save billions. But I guess you would rather spend all that money keeping all those bases there while fueling more hatred for America from the rest of the world. Yeah, I love paying more in taxes just to fuel politicians' military complex and terrorists' motivation to invade us. Although it is true that our military secures oil for Americans, it is immoral to use brute force to for economic interests. This also goes against the spirit of free market capitalism that America claims to stand for. Lastly, our long-term interest is that we gradually shift away from oil. Our dependence on oil pollutes the environment and increases the revenue for supporting terrorist activities. After all, the Middle East is where we get most of our oil, and the Middle East is the main source for financing terrorist. The rulers of many Middle Eastern countries get in power through their oil wealth, so it is very likely that their oil wealth helps them finance terrorism.

Okay, so if you don't want to withdraw military bases, can you at least stop sending military aid to other countries? We used to give biological and chemical weapons to Iraq to fight Iran, and now we view Iraq as our enemy. Currently, we give $3 billion per year in foreign aid to Israel, $1.8 billion of which is military while the other $1.2 billion is in economic aid. Oh, and now the US is giving Saudi Arabia military aid to counterbalance Iraq. I guess the fact that 15 out of the 19 terrorists who hijacked us on 9-11 are from Saudi Arabia shouldn't bother us. Saudi Arabia could easily go from being an ally to an enemy. Hell, maybe Israel may one day be our enemy. Military aid to other countries might haunt us. During the Cold War, we gave military aid to the Taliban of Afghanistan to fight against the Russians. Now Afghanistan is the headquarters for Al-Qaeda. Oh, and we talk about how Iraq is guilty of human rights abuses against its people. Well, Saudi Arabia is a very oppressive regime with few rights for citizens, especially women. Why not go to war with them? Because they are our partners, and we get oil from them.

Oh, and food aid isn't that helpful either. It puts local farmers in third world countries out of business because the people will get cheap or free food from the US rather than buying from their local farmers. Giving foreign aid in the form of technology may be useful, but military and food aid usually causes more problems than it solves.

Of course, not all our debt is caused by a wasteful foreign policy. We also have flawed domestic policies. Here's one piece of advice. Stop subsidizing big businesses like oil and farming. Last time I checked, you donate charity to the poor...not the rich. But maybe I'm just crazy. Okay, maybe you want to keep giving subsidies to big businesses that don't need that extra money. It's that "trickle-down" economy thing, right? Keep the rich even richer so they can use that money to create jobs? I definitely agree with giving the rich tax breaks, but the poor and middle class should also get tax breaks. In fact, we should get rid of income tax. But even if we don't get rid of income tax, it doesn't make sense to give special benefits to big businesses over the rest of the population.

The economy is in shambles, and unemployment is rising, so the "trickle-down economy" solution didn't work. I'm not sure if anybody told you, but it works both ways. The rich might hire the lower class and middle class, but the people lower on the economic ladder are customers for big businesses. For example, if the owner of Coca-Cola gets tax breaks , s/he may have more money to pay employees. However, somebody has to pay for the government's expenses. When the tax breaks are concentrated among the rich, that means the middle class and lower class have to pay a higher share of the taxes. The rich may provide jobs, but the poor and middle class buy from the rich. The more financially strapped they are, the harder it is for them to buy, which hurts big business. When they have lower taxes, they can buy more products from big companies like Hewlet-Packard, Apple, etc. So if the lower and middle class have more money, they can afford to buy more things from the rich. The economy is a cycle, not a pyramid. I guess you guys were asleep during that lesson in class.

President Obama seems to have a better grasp of this. He is reducing tax breaks to the rich and increasing tax breaks for the poor. However, increasing taxes on the rich is not solving the problem either. The government should reduce taxes on everybody. Although this will involve less government revenue, the government can still balance the budget if they stop spending so much money on wars, welfare programs, etc. Government can also take in revenue through donations if they do a good job.

Yearly US Budget Deficit or Surplus, 1961-2004 (in $Billions)

Clinton +523

| 1961 1962 | 1963-1968 | -1969-1974- | 1975 1976 | 1977-1980 | 1981-1988 | 1989-1992 | 1993-2000 | 2001-2004 |

$100

JFK -7   Johnson -18   Carter 0   126   127

Nixon +19

Ford -68

··Nixon-Ford·· -49

President Net Gain Net Loss

R Reagan -81

GHW Bush -135

projected 2003 -401

projected 2004 -480

GW Bush -713 FY 2004

Budget Data from **Congressional Budget Office** www.cbo.gov

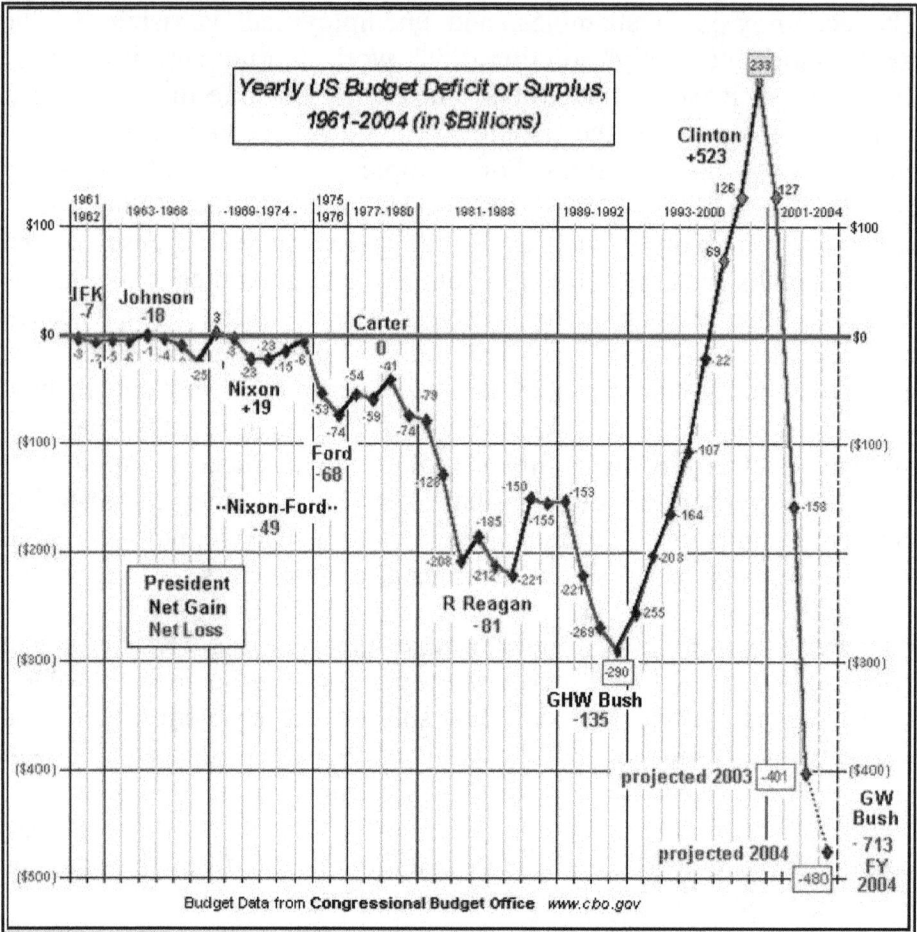

It might sound impossible for the US government to get out of debt, but there have been times in US history in which America has balanced the budget. The main period was during the second half of the Bill Clinton presidency. In the first half of Clinton's presidency, America's budget was still in a deficit, but during the early part of his second term, the budget was balanced. For the rest of the Clinton administration, the US Budget actually experienced a surplus. The surplus continued to rise rapidly, but started going down during the end of the Clinton administration. The US budget was still in a surplus, and continued to be a surplus even in the early part of the Bush Jr. administration. However, the surplus ended shortly after Bush Jr. went into office. In fact, it took a nose dive to a $400 billion deficit in 2004, primarily because of the Iraq war.

So although the US government traditionally has a history of spending more then it makes, it is still capable of balancing its budget and even having a surplus. It just needs to follow the same path as the Richard Nixon and Bill Clinton administration.

Now I also had this silly idea that getting rid of welfare would also help the economy. I kind of hate my tax money being used to give lazy bums a free home. I kind of thought that a better idea is to send them to Habitat for Humanity to help them build their own home and a homeless shelter to help them find a job. Or hell, maybe government can even give them job-training and even a government job in exchange for the home. That could save tax money, which will lower the national debit. But I guess the effort would be too much. Yeah, instead of helping these people get jobs, it's probably better to just give them free homes, free food, free everything, and no taxes while stealing that money from the rest of us hard-working Americans.

If you really want to be nice to Americans in addition to cutting the budget, there's a bunch of government agencies I would remove. Get rid of the IRS, Federal Reserve, US Department of Agriculture; they are so corrupt that their existence doesn't really help prevent businesses from practicing fraud. The National Cancer Institute is also unnecessary since we already have the American Cancer Society and many other nongovernmental charity organizations devoted to cancer.

The FDA is probably better off existing, but it also can be corrupt, so I advocate denationalizing it and turning it into a non-profit charity. Private companies can often become more corrupt than government organisations, but private nonprofit charities are much less corrupt than government organisations.

Another way for government to save money is to stop sending our tax money to support the International Monetary Fund and World Bank; again, nonprofit charities are much more qualified to help the poor than government organisations.

When the U.S. government provides food to developing nations, farmers in those countries go out of business because citizens in these countries don't purchase food from them. Also, the food that the U.S. government ships isn't always healthy, and there is no request from local agencies in those nations to receive the food aid. So this form of foreign aid seems very imperialistic. Nongovernmental agencies such as CARE help farmers grow food locally in their countries so they can produce more food for their families to eat and sell the food so they can financially support their families, thus creating jobs and fighting hunger. Medshare International is an agency that ships medical supplies overseas to developing countries. However, they have certain requirements before they send these supplies to hospitals abroad. First of all, they make sure the supplies are unused and haven't expired. Second of all, they make sure the hospitals in those countries request them. In other words, Medshare does not ship expired items, supplies that have already been opened, or products that have not been requested by hospitals.

Also, Medshare's work also has a positive impact on the United States. Many hospitals in America have excess medical supplies, and often times these unused medical supplies go in the landfill. But when American hospitals donate medical supplies that they have not used to Medshare instead of throwing them away, it helps keep our landfills from overflowing.

A New Role for the Military

Although the main job of the military is to provide defense, the US military can expand its role during peacetime. After all, if there is no war, it is a bad idea for the government to start wars just to give the military a use. It is also a bad idea for the military to become useless, so during peacetime, they can perform other roles. Because a military is skilled in technology, science, and other fields; they can improve the quality of life in poor areas. They can provide relief for areas that were hit by natural disasters. They can rebuild infrastructures. They can spread technology to the poor. Although this seems idealistic, there is also a practical benefit to this. When you help people get out of poverty, you help create customers. It is better to create customers by eliminating poverty than by using brute military force. The US Military is already involved in Toys For Tots. Maybe they should be involved in Computers for Africa. Computers for Africa is a nonprofit charity that provides computers to poor people in Africa, especially Uganda.

Although I generally do not advocate government being involved in foreign aid, as long as money is being spent on the military, it might as well be used in ways that reduce poverty. After all, a poor country is more likely to be run by a violent dictator than a rich one. A poor country is also more likely to be a breeding ground for terrorism, so this can be a nonviolent way for the military to protect America.

Complete libertarianism is an ideal that may not be possible to reach right now. So we should gradually head in that direction. Using the military to build infrastructure and spread technology in the third world will help the cause of free enterprise in the long run. By providing this infrastructure, that will make these poor countries become richer. They will more likely buy American products, which will benefit America's economy. They will also more likely practice capitalism because a rich population is harder for a government to control than a poor population.

The US military has done some important things throughout history. It freed America from the British, allowing America to be one of the freest societies in the world. It also helped get rid of the Nazis and Japanese during World War 2 (although American text books exaggerate America's role and ignore the role of China against the Japanese as well as Russia and England against the Nazis).

After World War 2, the American military has had a pretty unsuccessful history. The Vietnam War, Korean War, Gulf War, Somalian War, and the War in Iraq are all wars that did nothing to make America or the world any safer or freer. The reasons are hard to understand. Maybe one reason is that World War 2 pitted industrial countries against other industrial countries. When you devastate an industrial powerhouse like Germany or Japan, you shock them, which forces them to change. In the case of Vietnam, Korea, and Iraq, it doesn't help to devastate an already poor country. Also, right now, most countries with dictators are poor. Poverty makes it easier for dictators to take power. Bombing the hell out of a poor country will not remove a dictator. It keeps that country poor, making it easier for the dictator to stay in power. Even if you attack the dictator, you will attack innocents in the process, which the dictator can use to convince the poor that it is America's fault, not the dictator's fault. It only makes sense to attack a country if it attacked you first. No matter how bad the government is, it makes no sense to attack these countries if they do not attack you first.

I hate to admit that war is sometimes necessary. However, I think in the 21st century and beyond, we have less need of violence than we did in the past. Industrialized nations no longer go to war with each other. Right now, poor countries go to war with other poor countries, or rich nations go to war with poor nations. Poor countries also go to war with rich countries, usually in the form of terrorist attacks like September 11. There really is no incentive for 2 rich nations to go to war with each other. They have everything to lose and nothing to gain. I think the answer to bring world peace is not to get rid of the evildoers but to turn as many poor countries into rich countries as we can.

As for terrorists that attack the US, as much as I hate to admit it, some of our actions in the past motivate hatred. The US put the Shah of Iran in power against the will of the people. The US government provided Saddam Hussein with biological and chemical weapons to fight Iran. Not too long after that, the US went to war with Iraq because it invaded Kuwait. Although Iraq was acting immorally by invading Kuwait, why did the US have a problem with Iraq killing innocent

Kuwaitis but help Iraq kill innocent Iranians by providing Saddam Hussein weapons?

So what is the solution? Like I said, we should concentrate more on improving the infrastructure of poor countries. Now am I suggesting we get rid of our military? No, not at all. Unfortunately, we may need to use brute force if terrorists ever get their hands on nuclear and other weapons of mass destruction. However, we should put most of our efforts at killing the roots of terrorism rather than trying to kill the terrorists. The US military has many skills besides using weapons. It has state-of-the-art technology. The military can change its role to include things such as building schools, computer labs, and other areas for learning. Just as police officers direct traffic and work at the motor vehicle department in addition to dealing with crime, the US military can also diversify its role to include non-combat as well as combat operations. In fact, it should emphasize more on non-combat operations.

The CIA can also modify it's role. The CIA would have an easier time with this. After all, CIA stands for "Central Intelligence Agency." There is no part of that word that requires violence. Intelligence is about knowledge and information, so the CIA would be in the perfect position to provide computer and other educational infrastructure to poor countries. Heck, they could do that here in the US. There are still inner city schools and dirt-poor farming areas (especially in Alabama and Mississippi) that can benefit from better information technology.

Earth Freedom

America, Land of the Free?

While most nations are founded based on ethnicity, the United States of Amerca was founded upon an idea...freedom. The constitution mostly describes the rights of the people and the government's responsibility to protect that freedom. It does not talk a lot about the powers of the government over the people. Here are the first 10 Amendments of the Constitution.

First Amendment

Congress shall make no law respecting an establishment of religion, or prohibiting the free exercise thereof; or abridging the freedom of speech, or of the press; or the right of the people peaceably to assemble, and to petition the Government for a redress of grievances.

Second Amendment

A well regulated Militia, being necessary to the security of a free State, the right of the People to keep and bear Arms, shall not be infringed.

Third Amendment

No Soldier shall, in time of peace be quartered in any house, without the consent of the Owner, nor in time of war, but in a manner to be prescribed by law.

Fourth Amendment

The right of the people to be secure in their persons, houses, papers, and effects, against unreasonable searches and seizures, shall not be violated, and no warrants shall issue, but upon probable cause, supported by Oath or affirmation, and particularly describing the place to be searched, and the persons or things to be seized.

Fifth Amendment

No person shall be held to answer for any capital, or otherwise infamous crime, unless on a presentment or indictment of a Grand Jury, except in cases arising in the land or naval forces, or in the Militia, when in actual service in time of War or public danger; nor shall any person be subject for the same offence to be twice put in jeopardy of life or limb; nor shall be compelled in any criminal case to be a witness against himself, nor be deprived of life, liberty, or property, without due process of law; nor shall private property be taken for public use, without just compensation.

Sixth Amendment

In all criminal prosecutions, the accused shall enjoy the right to a speedy and public trial, by an impartial jury of the State and district where in the crime shall have been committed, which district shall have been previously ascertained by law, and to be informed of the nature and cause of the accusation; to be confronted with the witnesses against him; to have compulsory process for obtaining witnesses in his favor, and to have the Assistance of Counsel for his defense.

Seventh Amendment

In suits at common law, where the value in controversy shall exceed twenty dollars, the right of trial by jury shall be preserved, and no fact tried by a jury, shall be otherwise re-examined in any court of the United States, than according to the rules of the common law.

Eight Amendment

Excessive bail shall not be required, nor excessive fines imposed, nor cruel and unusual punishments inflicted.

Ninth Amendment

The enumeration in the Constitution, of certain rights, shall not be construed to deny or disparage others retained by the people.

Tenth Amendment

The powers not delegated to the United States by the Constitution, nor prohibited by it to the States, are reserved to the States respectively, or to the people.

Even though America is theoretically founded upon freedom, for most of America's history, it has only been free for a tiny percentage of the population. Women, African Americans, Native Americans, Catholics, Jews, and other minorities had no government protected rights for most of American history. Most African Americans were slaves. The US government and many early American citizens annihilated most Native American populations while kicking millions of others off of their homelands. Even minority white Americans such as the Irish were treated like second-class citizens. Women were treated as servants of their husbands. In fact, even among white, Anglo-Saxon Protestant men; the only ones that had rights were those that owned land. So even during America's development of the constitution,

America did not provide freedom for most Americans. It was probably better than the rest of the world, or at least most of the world, but it was still not free. Even today, there are many societies such as the Amish as well as many societies in Mississippi and Alabama that still oppress women, blacks, and other minorities.

Freedom to Deny Freedom?

Obviously, total freedom is a bad idea. We need rules and laws to protect citizens from rape, murder, theft, discrimination, fraud, etc. It makes no sense to argue for your right to murder because that denies somebody else's freedom to live. Likewise, it makes no sense to have freedom to rape others because that denies a woman, man, or child the freedom from unwanted sex. Stealing infringes upon a person's freedom of owning their own property while fraud infringes on a person's freedom of having true information. Traffic laws are used to provide people freedom of safety. So freedom only makes sense as long as it doesn't harm somebody else

America does a great job of defending such freedoms and protecting citizens against crimes. Although American police officers might not catch all criminals, violent and other crimes are taken seriously unlike many other countries. Bribery is relatively rare in the US. Nonetheless, there are police officers who practice police brutality and racism. By law, America is perfectly equal, but in practice, minorities still receive some unequal treatment. Even bribery happens in the US. Direct bribery to police officers in the US is rare, but many large corporations fund political campaigns to gain favors from politicians. This is very much a form of bribery. It is just less direct.

America also supports oppressive regimes in third world countries and has military bases all over the world. Occupying other nations against the will of the people while also supporting leaders who mistreat their people is not my idea of freedom.

Freedom of Marriage

Most Americans currently support the rights of women, racial minorities, religious minorities, and other groups. However, there is one group of people who the majority of Americans still have disrespect for...homosexuals. Although most Americans oppose violence against homosexuals, they still oppose their right to marriage. Of course, even though most Americans oppose violence against homosexuals, they are still indifferent to that violence. The news raises alarms during violence against women and racial minorities but largely ignores violence against homosexuals. Homosexuals currently suffer mistreatment.

Although the government does not violently persecute homosexuals, it bans homosexual marriage. Denying homosexuals the right to marry goes against freedom. Whether homosexually is wrong or right is a personal opinion, but it isn't the government's role to step in on this issue. My personal opinion is that there is nothing wrong with it. It does not harm anybody. Contrary to popular opinion, homosexuality does not cause AIDS. AIDS can only transfer between people who have AIDS, whether they are homosexual or heterosexual. Homosexuality is not a threat to society in any way, so preventing homosexuals from getting married does not serve the purpose of government. The government bans things like killing, stealing, fraud, rape, driving on a read light, and other crimes because it threatens the safety or welfare of other individuals. There is no reason for people to have the freedom to kill, steal, or rape because these actions threaten the safety and freedom of other individuals. However, homosexuality does not threaten anybody's safety. Yes, it is true that males who molest boys are committing a crime (and so are women molesting girls). However, it is also a crime for males to molest girls, and it is a crime for women to molest boys. If two adults males or adult females have sex with each other and give consent, there is nothing criminal or even immoral about the act. Society is quick to blame homosexuals for child molestation even though most child molestors are heterosexual.

In addition, there is no logical reason why two spouses should get tax cuts just because they happen to be different genders while the homosexual couple pays more in taxes. There is nothing constitutional about this practice and I see no reason to add a constitutional amendment to ban gay marriage. Homosexuality is not harmful at all. In fact, because homosexuals cannot have babies of their own, they often adopt.

If more homosexual couples adopt children, this would reduce the number of children that live in orphanages. Not only does this save taxpayers money that the government uses to maintain orphanages and feed orphans, but adoption also provides homes for these orphans. Some argue that a homosexual couple is not able to provide the care of a heterosexual couple. Others argue that a homosexual couple will always provide poor care for children. Even if heterosexuals provide better care than a homosexual couple does, a homosexual couple will provide a better life than an orphanage. As far as homosexuals providing poor care and being harmful to the child, these are merely irrational fears based on false beliefs rather than evidence.

Banning homosexual marriage is a denial of freedom and also very impractical. Because homosexuals cannot have children, they can adopt children, which will take children away from orphanages and into homes. This will give the orphans more opportunity, and it will save American tax dollars on orphanages. Nonetheless, I don't see how we can call ourselves free if we cannot free ourselves from holding on to traditions that have absolutely no benefit. Allowing homosexuals to marry will benefit society, yet we want to ban it because of our own personal opinions. In some cases, other countries have more freedom than the US. In many European countries, homosexual marriage is protected by law. In many parts of Europe, society has more marital freedom. In the US, even now, most people are expected to marry. If they are not married, society pressures them to hurry up and find somebody. In Europe, there is much less of that. There is more freedom to stay single and also to cohabitate.

Political Freedom

Some other countries have more freedom in terms of political parties. Other nations have also had heads of state from minority religions. India has had Manmohan Singh, a Sikh, as a prime minister. Jawaharlal Nehru was atheist, yet he was the first prime minister of India. Although some of America's founding fathers were either atheist or deist, currently, it would be nearly impossible to be a US president without being a member of a Christian church. No matter how qualified a candidate is, a Jew, Muslim, Buddhist, Hindu, or atheist will not become a US president any time soon. However, in parts of Africa, you can have heads of state that are Muslim, Christian, or even tribal. Although India has a mostly Hindu population, it currently has a Sikh prime minister...Manmohan Singh. India's first prime minister Jawaharlal Nehru was atheist. How is it that America, the most diverse country in the world, can fall behind such traditional societies such as India in terms of respecting religious diversity. How can we call it freedom when the president of our country has to be affiliated with a specific religion? Although the US government does not legally prohibit minority religions from becoming president, freedom also has to do with freedom of society. A society that absolutely refuses to vote a non-Christian president is not really free.

Some countries have had a woman head of state. Indira Gandhi was prime minister of India. Indira Gandhi inherited the title some time after her father Jawaharlal Nehru died rather than being elected, so this situation does not count. However, in many other cases, the woman head of state was elected. Benazzir Bhutto was elected as prime minister of Pakistan. Golda Meir was elected president of Israel. England elected Margaret Thatcher as her prime minister. The US has never elected a woman head of state.

Of course, America is still much freer than most countries. I have no complaints about my freedom. I am very lucky to be born in the US and live in this country. However, despite being lucky, I think it would be false to say that America is the beacon of freedom. American freedom is great but has its limitations. Also, freedom is not uniquely American. Freedom as a global ideal instead of an American or Western value. You cannot confine ideas such as freedom to a geographic area. Freedom is freedom regardless of where it is practiced. Some areas may represent freedom more than others. Europe and America may have more freedom than Africa and Asia. Of course, there are also many people in Africa and Asia that are freer than certain areas of America and Europe. For example, Shanghai must be a freer place to live than rural Alabama or many inner-city areas of the US. And, as mentioned earlier, America has only been this free very recently. In addition, America's concept of freedom is influenced by other cultures.

Democracy and Greek Philosophy

It is still a good example for other countries to follow America to improve their living standards. However, America did not create the idea of democracy. It was largely influenced by ancient Greek philosophy. The word democracy even comes from the Greek words "demos" which means people, and "ocracy" which means "rule." So the idea of America being a government "ruled by the people" was influenced by ancient Greek philosophers such as Plato. In fact, the city of Athens followed a direct democracy in which civilians directly participated in government, while America still has a representative democracy in which people elect members of government but have no say on the law after voting. The American judicial system was influenced by the Athenian judicial system. The trial process involved philosophers making arguments about the innocence or guilt of a convicted felon. These philosophers were equivalent to defense and prosecution attorneys.

It would be a mistake to say that ancient Greece was truly free. Women were not allowed to participate in the direct democracy of Athens. About one third of Greek society were slaves, so ancient Greece was by no means totally free. Nonetheless, millions of African Americans were slaves for much of American history, so the US was not much better than Greece in that respect. The concepts of democracy such as trial using evidence for convicting criminals, voting for leaders (instead of leaders using violence to take power), and other democratic principles came from Greece and did not originate in America.

Freedom and the Rising Sun

Other cultures have also influenced America's political ideas. While many countries have kings and other hereditary titles, positions in the US government are elected rather than given the title by birth (well, with the possible exeption of George W. Bush, son of previous president George H.W. Bush, who may have won in a rigged election involving his brother in Florida).

The Chinese philosopher Kung Fu Tzu (AKA Confucius), started the practice of requiring government officials to pass examinations.

Usually, political positions were given to the sons of men in high positions or people who use brute force. Even today this is common, so Kung Fu Tzu was way ahead of his time. Kung Fu Tzu did advocate that people obey and honor their rulers, but he also promoted the idea that rulers should serve their people.

Although Kung Fu Tzu promoted a strict separation of classes and statuses, he let go of those statuses when teaching. Even though he didn't promote equality at all times, he did promote it in his classroom. Below is a verse from one of his books.

"In teaching, there should be no distinction of classes." Analects XV, 39

Although Kung Fu Tzu promoted some concepts of political freedom, Kung Fu Tzu's ideas were not perfect. He still promoted a man's superiority over his wife and children. Kung Fu Tzu suggested that the man treat his wife and children with respect, but he still viewed the man as superior. Even though Kung Fu Tzu had flaws, he still made a great contribution to the practice of freedom.

Holy Cow; Kings of Freedom

Although Indian history is filled with the caste system and other forms of discrimination, some of India's rulers have contributed to the freedom of the people. The Buddhist emperor Ashok originally spread his empire through violence, but after converting to Buddhism, he took efforts to bring peace to his kingdom. Ashok outlawed animal sacrifice and established veterinarian hospitals. He also established universities to allow people to learn and built irrigation systems.

The Mughal Empereror Abu Akbar also contributed to India's freedom. During the Mughal empire, there was a special tax on Hindus that Muslims didn't have to pay. Akbar removed this tax. Akbar also created dialogues for people of different religions to discuss their ideas rather than killing each other in the name of religion. Of course, it is important to take note that although Akbar improved the condition of Hindus during the Mughal Empire, he also destroyed Hindu temples and waged jihad against Hindu kings. Perhaps he wanted freedom of religion as long as India is still ruled under Islam. Despite his great flaws, he still improved freedom for India's people. If the Muslim world was ruled by leader like Akbar the Great.

A Free World

The whole concept of America or any other country being the "land of freedom" is very out-of-date. To truly be free, we have to go beyond political boundaries. We need to be united not as nations but as a world. Although we can still have nations, our main loyalty should be to the world, and loyalty to our nation comes second. Nations should be more like states. I am not necessarily talking about re-organizing the world politically but rather in our hearts and minds. The world was once a giant continent called Pangaea over hundreds of millions years ago. Although the continents are now separated geographically, we can still unite economically and socially.

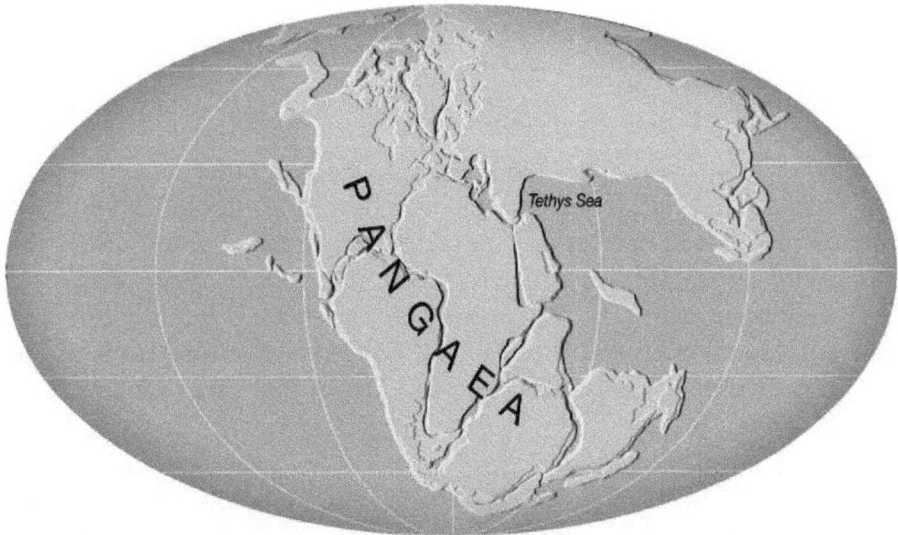

Most countries in Western Europe have a lot of freedom. They have similar political rights as America. Japan, South Korea, and Taiwan are industrialized, democratic countries as well. Freedom is by no means uniquely American or western. Most other parts of the world are not completely free, but they are improving. Many countries in Latin America and sub-Saharan Africa are improving their freedom record. Ghana is a stable country. After the new leader of Rwanda took power after the genocide, the Rwandan government is using its resources to spread fiber computers and Internet technology all over the country. The Rwandan government currently is relatively free of corruption. In Latin American, countries like Brazil and Venezuela are doing well. Although much of Africa and Latin America are plagued by violence, things are improving.

Before we can consider the world free, we must work together to make it free. Poor countries such as Burma or much of sub-Saharan Africa will not magically become free. They need to be lifted out of poverty to become free. Donating to charity organizations that improve the economy is one way. CARE provides economic development to poor countries. They not only help farmers produce more food but also help business in those countries grow. You can learn more about CARE at www.careusa.org. Computers For Africa is an organization that provides computer technology in Africa, especially to Uganda. Their website is http://computers4africa.org/.

Animal Freedom

When talking about freedom, we usually speak about freedom for humans. However, we don't speak much about freedom for other living creatures. While America currently has a great record of freedom for humans, it has a horrible record of treating animals. American factory farms kill billions of animals every year. It is not the killing itself but rather the confined conditions that make factory farms a crime against life.

Of course, farms chose to be factory farms rather than free-range because it saves money. To encourage farms to become free range, the government can give tax breaks to free range farms and stop subsidizing factory farms.

Killing for food is a part of the natural cycle, so it won't make sense to illegalize the meat industry. If we prohibit humans from eating meat, then we should do the same for lions, monkeys, and other creatures. Although monkeys can survive without meat, lions would die out. However, it wouldn't make much sense to allow lions to eat meat but ban humans from doing so. So making it illegal to kill for food would not be a very practical law.

One concern is that if we allow humans to kill other animals for food, why not allow them to kill each other for food. This is a sensible question. Allowing cannibalism would be very impractical and greatly harm civilization. After all, lions don't eat other lions; they eat other creatures. Likewise, it wouldn't make sense to allow humans to kill each other for food but not each other. Many homocides could be justified because the murderer would eat the murder victim. This would be a bad idea.

Although killing other animals for food should not be a legal crime, it is still good as a moral principal to consume as little as possible. Similar to monkeys and chimps, we do not need animal flesh for survival. We can survival on plant food alone. Plant foods are generally a poor source of vitamin B12, but multi-vitamins can supply these. It is a good idea to minimize the amount of suffering we cause, and reducing our consumption of animal products can reduce the demand for killing animals or putting them in factory farms. Eating animal products itself does not cause them to be killed, but buying animal products creates demand for abusing farm animals. It would be nice if lions could survive on a vegetarian diet, but they can't. Nonetheless, even though some creatures require animal flesh for survival, it is still a good idea to make an effort to reduce even further animal suffering.

Sources Cited

Cartledge, Paul (2001). The Democratic Experiment
http://www.bbc.co.uk/history/ancient/greeks/greekdemocracy_01.shtml

Ven. S. Dhammika (1993). "The Edicts of King Ashok." The Wheel Publication No. 386/387
http://www.cs.colostate.edu/~malaiya/ashoka.html

Crime and Punishment

Moral Codes

As important it is to be free, freedom has its limits. We should not be free to do something that violates anybody else's rights. Rape, killing, stealing, and other acts are violations of somebody else's freedom. Society came of with punishments to discourage people who commit crimes. Throughout history, society wrote moral codes to regulate the behavior of the population. Ideally, it would be good if everybody got what he or she wanted, but different people have conflicting interests. In some cases, people kill other people for territory, money, land, and other goods. Other people steal goods. Rape is another crime in which one person's desires conflict with another. The man who wants sex may rape a woman to satisfy his desires, but he is causing harm to the woman. Moral codes prohibit killing, stealing, or other actions that cause harm to other people. Some moral codes extend this concern for life to prohibit harming other animals.

The most important rule of morality is the Hippocratic Oath...Do No Harm. This is not a perfect rule. Sometimes it is necessary to harm others for the greater good. For example, it is necessary to kill people like Hitler, Osama Bin Ladin, and other mass-murders to preserve the lives of innocent people. By eating food, we cause harm to plants and animals, but it would be impossible to survive by giving up food, so it is best to eat food in a way that causes minimal harm to other living creatures while keeping you healthy. Although it is sometimes necessary to harm other beings to survive, in most cases, we should avoid doing things that harm others. Morality goes beyond avoiding actions that harm yourself and others. We should also try to spread the most amount of happiness for the most people. Some things that give happiness also cause harm. It is wrong to inflict harm on others by killing, raping, insulting, or other deeds regardless of how much happiness it gives you. There are also subtle pleasures that cause harm. Although eating candy gives happiness, too much candy leads to health problems such as heart disease, high blood pressure, and lethargy. In addition, avoiding work to go to parties leads to temporary enjoyment, but it causes long-term harm. It is impossible to give an exact code for all moral actions, but the best guideline is to spread the most amount of happiness with the minimum amount of suffering.

Tough on Crime

American law is noteworthy in that it views a defendant as innocent until proven guilty. The discovery of DNA further allowed the judicial system to find evidence for guilt or innocence. America is also noteworthy for freedoms that many nations do not have. Women have all of the legal privileges as men. All races in the US have equal legal rights as well. The US also has a system of checks and balances that reduces the risk of any one political leader from having too much power. Citizens in the US have freedom of religion or freedom to have no religion, which many nations do not provide. Lastly, the US allows citizens to express grievances to the government without execution or imprisonment.

Although I mostly agree with America's stance on freedom, I do believe the US has a lenient method of punishing rapists and violent criminals. People who are guilty of such crimes should not be put in jail for a temporary time and be let out. They will most likely commit those crimes again. People generally do not hire ex-cons. Because these ex-cons are not able to find work, they see no way to make a living other than going back to prison, so they commit crimes again. This puts society in great danger. A better solution is to keep them in jail, but supervise them performing a public service. This way, keeping them alive through taxpayer money at least has some benefit.

Although prisons are not a convenient way to live, they are much more comfortable than the life a criminal lives outside of prison. In jail, criminals are fed well, and they get free exercise facilities. Even though they are at risk of being raped in prison, their lives are much harder outside of prison on the streets.

If the government does not put criminals to use, then it is better to execute them than to keep them alive on taxpayer money. It is much better to remove the criminal from the planet to prevent them from committing more crimes against humanity then to keep them in jail and release them and allow them to commit such crimes. Of course, a criminal who comes from a life of poverty and physical abuse may prefer death to staying out of jail in a harsh life. In such cases, it seems torture would be a much more useful punishment to prevent violent criminals than simply executing them. I am not sure if I would actually advocate torture as punishment, but it would certainly be more effective in preventing violent crime than simple execution.

Although punishment is a necessary evil, prevention is a better weapon against crime. We should look at the areas and circumstances where criminals arise, and then try to root out those problems. An upbringing in poverty is one of the things that leads to crime. People may steal out of desperation, or they may sell drugs. Although selling drugs in and of itself a violent crime, because many drugs are illegal, people from desperate backgrounds may sell them on the streets. Gang wars to maintain drug supply and territory is common in such areas, so reducing poverty is one way to prevent crime in such areas. Organisations such as Boys & Girls Club and After School All-stars also provide activities in inner-city areas that are at risk for crime. Volunteering for such organisations can be one way to help.

Vice City

While the US is too lenient in punishing criminals, it also makes things illegal that should be legal. Sometimes they include business activities that hurt the buyer, but the buyer but doesn't harm anybody else, and the buyer should be fully aware of the risks. These are often called victimless crimes because the customer is buying a service out of his or her free will. Banning prostitution, marijuana, and abortion are ineffective at preventing these actions. People do not stop smoking marijuana because it is illegal. They often do so because they are unhappy with their lives. The risk of going to jail will not prevent most people from smoking marijuana. In fact, making it illegal allows an unregulated black market to thrive. The US once prohibited alcohol. It did not prevent people from drinking alcohol, but it did cause organized crime agencies to thrive on selling alcohol illegally. Gang wars also arise among groups that sell drugs illegally. This occurs now with cocaine. Many gangs shoot and kill each other to remove competition from their drug trade. By making them legal, they can sell these drugs in stores and not on the streets. In addition, we should try to find out what causes people to sell drugs in the first place and help them find a better way to live their lives while also doing the same for people who take drugs. Many people who enter the drug trade are poor and live on the streets, so fighting poverty is one possible way to prevent the sale of drugs.

In addition to economic policies, we also have needless laws that cost us unnecessary money in law enforcement. In other words, we should only make things illegal such as stealing, fraud, killing, rape, and other things that deny people's rights. For example, I don't agree with laws against marijuana, cocaine, and prostitution. I personal don't agree with these actions, but if the buyer and seller are doing these transaction with consent and without violence, I see no reason to ban them.

Oh, what's that? You are worried that if you legalize prostitution, people will go to prostitutes? If we legalize marijuana and cocaine, it will cause people to take them? Well, call me crazy, but last time

I checked, people don't avoid drugs and prostitution because they are illegal. But maybe I'm wrong. Maybe, if we try really, really hard at making them illegal, one day nobody will take them. There must be millions of people who decide not to take cocaine or marijuana because the government says it's bad. What about those people who already take them? Oh, maybe they don't know it's illegal. Maybe I need to go tell them. Then they'll stop, right? It couldn't be because they know it's illegal but take drugs anyway?

Sorry guys...I just had this crazy idea that the government can save money if they stop spending so much money paying cops to hunt down and arrest marijuana and cocaine users who aren't harming anybody. I just thought that maybe, if you made these drugs legal, you would save money on paying cops and make money by taxing these drug dealers. After all, if marijuana and cocaine dealers had legitimate businesses, they would have to pay for a business license and pay taxes. That's what you guys do to the tobacco industry and alcohol industry. Oh, I guess tobacco and alcohol don't really cause any harm. I guess you guys don't want to save money and make some extra cash so you can reduce your debt, right? You'd probably rather have these pot dealers and crack dealers make money without paying taxes. Yeah, you're right. It's better that these guys do their business underground and on the streets where it is hard to regulate, and you've got gang violence from turf wars over who gets to sell on what side of the street. I haven't heard of turf wars over tobacco and alcohol. Oh, but I guess that's a shame. After all, these turf wars create jobs for cops, right?

Prostitution is legal in the Netherlands, France, Nevada, and many other places. I thought that maybe if the rest of America legalizes prostitution, we can save even more money from paying cops to patrol streets to arrest hookers and pimps. If prostitution becomes a legal business, then...yeah, that's right...they will have to pay taxes, too. Oh, and if prostitution was legal, than it can be regulated so that the businesses can do tests on their clients to make sure they are free from STDs. Spend less money, collect more in taxes, and keep society safer...sound good? Okay, maybe not. Maybe you're right. Keeping prostitution illegal will eventually put it to an end. Yeah, that's right. Good thinking Uncle Sam.

Banning prostitution does not prevent women from becoming prostitutes. It just forces prostitutes and pimps to work underground. This actually does more harm than legalizing prostitution. Pimps often physically abuse their prostitutes while hording most of the money for themselves. If prostitution becomes legal, prostitutes will experience treatment, and they collect more money. There are already escort services in the US in which escorts get paid fairly well and do not experience the mistreatment by pimps. Escort services are legal because they charge money for dates rather than sex, but in reality, the dates end up involving sex. So escort services are basically prostitution companies that found a loophole to avoid getting cops to arrest them. If prostitution became legal, it would function like escort services. This means they can regulate for STDs and prostitutes will be treated much better. Because we will never remove prostitution, why not legalize it and make it safer?

Abortion is another action that causes harm, but it should stay legal because making it illegal causes more harm than good. Although abortion involves the killing of a fetus, it is debatable how conscious a foetus is. By having an abortion, it is possible that a potential mother will be spared from living a harsh life of taking care of a child that she is unable to care for. In addition, improper care can lead to disastrous results for the child. Most women who have abortions are poor and do not have access to birth control, so they often become pregnant without actually desiring a baby. The children of poor, single women often become criminals, thus abortion can prevent would-be criminals from being born. This sounds cruel, but it is wrong to deny facts no matter how harsh they sound. It is true that they would not be pregnant if they controlled their behavior and abstained from sex, but preaching about the benefits of abstinence will not prevent people from acting on their urges. Also, we must not forget that the man also had sex with that woman, so he also should control his desires. In fact, many of these men abandon their children and the mother of the children, so we should put more pressure on the men.

In addition, many women who have abortions are victims of rape, thus their pregnancy is not the result of voluntary behavior. In this case, we should not only find out why some men rape women, but also educate women on how to prevent themselves form being raped. If a rapist sees a woman with a large group of friends and/or family, they are unlikely to rape the woman. The woman's friends or family can fight off the criminal. Even if the rapist has a gun, the family and friends can attack the rapist while he is on top of the woman. The man cannot rape the woman and hold a gun simultaneously. Therefore, the criminal would think twice before raping a woman traveling in a group. However, if a woman travels alone, the rapist feels he is more likely to get away with the crime.

Making abortion illegal does not prevent abortions; it forces women to find other ways to have abortions such using coat hangers in a back alley. Although abortion is legal in this country, many American citizens as well as members of Congress, want to overturn Roe v. Wade. I do not like abortion at all, and I firmly advocate any social reform that can prevent abortions. Many poor women do not have knowledge about where they can get birth control, so this can be a step to prevent them from getting pregnant in the first place rather than worry about whether we should allow them to have abortions. Of course, birth control is still not 100% affective, and some pregnancies result even when a couple uses birth control. However, if the poor use birth control, there will be a large reduction in the number of unwanted babies even.

Eco Law

In addition to human minorities, non-human animals experience mistreatment. I do not suggest we give other animals the right to vote, nor would I put illegalize hunting. However, there should be laws against unnecessary cruelty to animals. Most meat, eggs, and dairy products in this country come from factory farming. Only free-range animal products should be allowed. Animal testing should also have limitations or maybe be abolished. Many medical tests can be done safely on humans. For those that are not safe, we can perform the tests on criminals rather than innocent animals. Not only is this more fair, but results would be more accurate.

Many people believe humans are naturally superior to other animals. Therefore, we have a right to use them for our purposes. First, I would like to repeat that I do not oppose hunting, nor do I oppose free- range animal products.

It is debatable whether eating meat is natural or unnatural. On the one hand, humans cannot eat most raw meat safely; we did not eat meat until we discovered fire. On the other hand, modern humans (i.e. Homo sapiens) did not discover fire. Our ancestors, the Homo erectus discovered fire. Even before discovering fire, they still ate insects without cooking, although insects probably made a small percentage of their diet. Although the Australopithecus Afarensis and other hominid ancestors ate a plant-based diet, they were not technically modern humans. Most primates are omnivores, although their diet is has very small amounts of animal flesh, and most of this flesh comes from insects. Currently, humans cannot get vitamin B12 from plants. They must either consume animal products or vitamin B12 supplements such as multi-vitamins and fortified cereals. However, vitamin B12 actually comes from bacteria rather than animals. Most animals flesh has the bacterium cynobalamin, which the main source of vitamin B12 for humans. Plants sometimes absorb this bacterium from their soil. However, modern farming involves washing away plants, which often removes the bacteria. Failure to rinse-off the plants may lead to health problems, so it may be a bad idea to eat plants that are not washed. Multi-vitamins are the best way to get vitamin B12 if you consume a vegan diet.

It does not really matter whether something is natural or unnatural but rather if it causes harm or benefit. Birth control is not natural, but it prevents millions of unwanted births and thus reduces poverty. Medical advances are not natural, but they save many lives. Automobiles and computers are not natural, but they unite the world, speed-up services,

Similar to environmental conservation, reducing animal suffering does not have to be an all-or-nothing decision. We can reduce consumption of animal products rather than eliminate it from our diets to reduce animal suffering. We can also limit ourselves to eating free-range meat, eggs, and dairy products or consume free-range most of the time.

Many economic activities such as logging destroy animals homes. Some activities kill animals and even wipe out species. It is impractical to prohibit such activities because it will not stop these industries. However, we should take action. Increased funding for alternative fuels is one idea. In addition, I believe the government should ban cruel forms of factory farming. All farming should be free-range. Perhaps the government should limit the number of farm animals per a given number of acres. If the government does not place such laws, we can chose to only buy dairy products, eggs, and meat made from free-range farms, or we can chose to only buy vegetarian food. Rather than restrict loggers from cutting down trees, they should be required or encouraged to replant the trees. Many laws protect lands by making national parks. Of course, we cannot rely on the government for everything. We can chose to volunteer for organizations that plant trees.

Government and Free Enterprise

I consider myself libertarian. Government is best that governs least. The government has a very important role in defending our rights such as freedom from theft, rape, fraud, etc. It also can license businesses and give patents. Military is also necessary (i.e. freedom from outside invaders). However, regulating the economy is not what the government is for. When government tries to get involved in welfare, foreign aid, and other economic issues, they usually do a bad job. Non-government organizations are better for this job.

Welfare

Tax-funded welfare programs are a disaster. Non-government charities such as Habitat for Humanity and homeless shelters do a much better job of helping the poor. Although I generally do not like government being involved in social welfare, one thing the government can do is be an intermediary to take poor people to nongovernment charity organizations. Because government has access to information that nobody else does, they can easily find people in need and then take them to charities. Maybe the government's job should take people who are in need and place them in such programs. However, the government should not provide food and shelter with taxpayer money. All this does is keep these people lazy for the rest of their lives. It also eat-ups taxpayer money, increases the national debt, and keeps welfare recipients from becoming successful. Nonprofit charities, on the other hand, take voluntary donations and use them to help poor people actually get jobs and no longer stay stuck in poverty. Of course, there will be those who are still stuck in poverty either by choice or by circumstances no matter how effective a charity organization helps, but non government charities consistantly do a better job than goverment welfare. So government can help by transferring people in need to organizations like Habitat for Humanity and then let these organizations provide the welfare.

Financial Sector

The bailout sucks. It is socialism for the rich. Letting big businesses fall will be painful at first, but it will teach them lessons that will help them improve later. After all, small businesses don't get a bailout when they fail. They go out of business or get bought out. The same rule should apply to big businesses. The US government's bailout of the financial industry is corporate welfare.

"YEAH, YEAH, THIS IS JUST TEMPORARY... THE FREE MARKET WORKS BEST WHEN THERE'S NO GOVERNMENT INTERVENTION... GET IN LINE, BUDDY!"

Oil and Other Lobbyists

Although I usually am against taxes, I would support a higher gas tax because driving involves using the roads, which is a service that the government provides. The more you buy gas, this means the more you drive, so you aren't just charged a tax based on how much income or profit you make. Having higher toll booths may be another way for government to generate more tax revenue as an alternative to income tax.

Government should stop subsidizing meat, grain, and oil. The government is not providing a public service by making these items cheaper. There would be a lot less obesity if meat and dairy products were more expensive. Of course, it isn't the government's right to force people to eat healthy. However, if these products are cheap only because of government subsidies, then this means government is intervening, which is a violation of free enterprise.

I can see how government may need to subsidize the use of solar energy and other environmentally-friendly technologies, but subsidizing bio-diesel is one reason why food prices are going so high. Actually, bio-diesel itself is responsible for the rising prices of food, but government subsidies make it worse. Although bio-diesel might not cause an increase in air pollution, it involves clearing land, which is a form of environmental destruction. Although I believe the private sector is a better way to strengthen solar energy and other green technologies, I am willing to accept government subsidies for green technologies if they provide them to replace subsidies for oil. As long as government subsidizes somebody, it should at least be industries that benefit the planet rather than make it worse. Of course, the government doesn't have to prevent people from polluting the environment, but it also shouldn't subsidize pollution.

Wall Street and Banks

Although many people blame the financial crisis on lack of regulation, many people have a few misconceptions about the free market. Selling real estate loans and investments is a form of fraud. Under free enterprise, the government still has a right to intervene if a company practices fraud.

Many people say lack of government regulation lead to the financial crisis. In fact, government intervention is part of the reason (but not the only reason) for the financial crisis. The US government was largely responsible for getting Fannie Mae to give loans to people who couldn't afford it. The US government is also responsible for printing lots of paper money, which is part of the reason for inflation.

The Federal Reserve regulates interest rates. Right now, they are trying to lower interest rates to get so Americans will take out more loans and keep banks in business. This also means people are getting less interest in their savings accounts. A bank should be able to charge whatever interest rate it wants as long as it provides that information to the applicant before s/he signs the loan. Banks also do not have the right to change the interest rate after the loan is signed unless this is agreed upon by the loan applicant. In other words, one year after giving a loan, the bank should not be allowed to increase the interest unless the loan recipient was informed about this before signing the application. You can argue that if banks could charge whatever they want, they would charge 24% interest. However, this would be bad business because they would have trouble getting people to sign take loans.

Holding Government Accountable

The government also has to pay its staff such as the President and members of Congress. Although this is legitimate, the government should not raise taxes in order to increase the salaries of politicians. Just like any company, the government should fire politicians who act unethically or fail at their job. If George W. Bush worked for a company, he would be fired for his failed policies. He may even go to jail. Being a politician should not protect his job. He should be fired.

The majority of actions in government are really just meetings and speeches. A small percentage of government time involves real action and passage of laws. Imagine a company that spends 90% of its time having board meetings; well, that's a lot like government. If there is very little being accomplished, then the government should have no problem laying off people in Congress. If sales are low in a business, it might lay people off to survive. The government should do the same thing.

Even though the free market can cause financial crises, the government usually gets in the way of helping the free market fix its problems. When government controls many industries, they become very inefficient and resistant to change. Just look at public schools. Government's role in the economy should be to make sure companies do not cheat their customers. And of course, government should arrest any company that uses violence to maintain their business. However, government should never actually tell a business what it should do, and government should never give a failing company money to save itself.

Freedom of Education

Family Choice

School is another institution that the government should have less control over. We often hear that America is a free country, but education is one area where it is more socialist than free. If you want to start a school and teach however you want, you will not be able to do so. If I want to start a school based on this technology, business, and charity; the government will not let me. I have to go through an accreditation process. I will have to teach the subjects that the government thinks is important. I am sure the government will have no problem if I teach business and technology. However, I will also have to teach a certain number of years of history, grammar, etc. I cannot decide to eliminate history and grammar. It should be the parents, not the government, who decides whether a school gives a proper education.

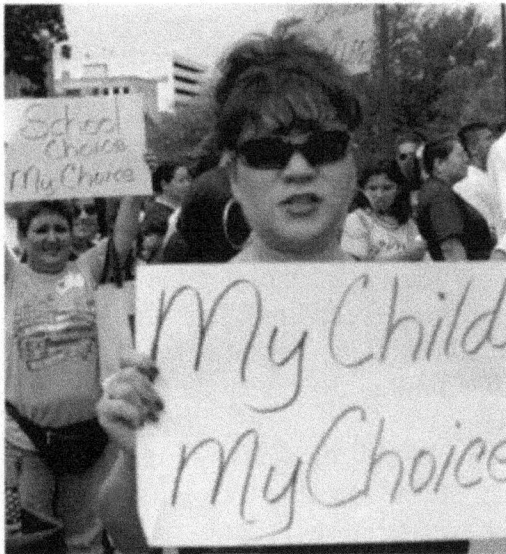

So if traditional schools want to keep teaching how they teach, that's fine. However, I should be able to start my own school with very little government interference. I can understand if government regulates education if I want to start a medical school or teach any form of healthcare. Parents and their children should be protected from schools that teach quack healthcare. However, for matters that do not directly deal with health or life and death, there should be less regulations.

So if I start my own school, and parents think the traditional educational system is better for their children, that's their right. Maybe I will go out of business because I can't attract these students. It isn't my right to force the government to keep me in business by any means. It isn't the government's job to force parents to send their children to my school just because they happen to live in that area. Likewise, the government has no right to regulate most other formats on education.

Although it is true that parents can send their children to private schools or even home school their children, the government still decides the subjects that are taught. Children still have to take regular standardized tests with standards set by the government. A certified teacher evaluates if the parents are teaching subjects that are also taught in public and private schools. Again, it is the job of schools to decide what to teach their students, and parents have the option to keep their children in another school if they don't like what a school teaches. If parents want to home school their children, they should be able to chose what subjects to teach their children.

In addition to giving parents freedom to decide what education is right for their children, students have the right to make sure that parents don't abuse this privilege. For example, parents may own a business. Parents do not have the right to limit their children's education by only teaching things to continue the business. Students should be free to do careers that they want rather than what their parents' chose for them.

Of course, there should still be some regulation on what schools can teach. A school should not be able to teach medicine however it feels like. It would be wrong if a school performs dangerous medical experiments however they feel like. They should not have medical schools for 8 year olds. Schools should not make 6 year olds do any kind of factory work or manual labor. Anything that jeopardizes the safety and health of students should not be allowed. However, a school should have the right to replace traditional schools subjects with sales, technology, and other classes that it feels are more practical.

We often hear that education is the key to our career, but in reality, schools can be a barrier to success. Although basic reading, writing, and math skills are very important; most of everything else we learn in schools is useless in our careers. Lawyers, doctors, accountants, and scientists depend on school for their career; but most other people have a career that is very different from what they learned in school. Schools should have more freedom to decide their own curriculum. If a school doesn't want to teach history, it shouldn't have to. Parents care for the welfare of their children, and if all schools became private, then schools would have to compete against each other. Many people think that private schools would be too expensive. Private school is expensive largely because there are so few of them. However, if there were more of them, they would become cheaper, especially if taxpayer money used to support schools was given back to Americans. Charter schools and other independent schools already charge much less than traditional private schools.

Some people may think that having government regulate schools makes them more accountable, but having government control schools actually makes them less accountable. After all, why do private schools consistantly outperform public schools? Part of it may be that students in private schools have wealthy parents who can provide them with better resources. However, the main reason is that a private school that disappoints it's students (or their parents) may go out of business. If a public school disappoints students and parents, it can still stay in business as long as the government doesn't decide to shut it down.

Of course, children may not know the value of money, especially since their parents are paying for school rather than them. Although children and parents should be like customers, schools should have more control so that they can prevent students from being disruptive. Parents cannot always make their children stop misbehaving. Private schools are much better than public schools in enforcing discipline. They sometimes beat children for misbehavior. A child who is told to leave class for misbehavior probably won't change their ways, but a child who is punished with beating might change. Of course, violence should be a last resort. A child should not be bruised or bleed; a slap on the hand is okay. A better solution may be to make the child do push-ups or manual labor for misbehaving. Another solution is not just to rely on punishment but to make school more interactive. Although I do not agree with misbehavior, part of why students disrupt class is that they really see no reason why they should be forced to sit-down, shut-up, and listen to things that they see no benefit of. Little children are biologically made to move around and interact rather than just sit down. Teenagers have raging hormones, so again, having them sit down and listen is unnatural. Having interactive activities in education will reduce misbehavior because it doesn't fight natural tendencies. In jobs, shutting up doesn't work. Of course, misbehavior will get you fired, but managers and staff still interact and exchange ideas. Managers and owners may have more authority, but other staff are still part of the communication process.

Of course, one problem with this is that poor people may not have access to a good education. They may not be able to afford it. There are a few possible solutions. Schools can give lower-priced or free education to the poor. They can collection donations similar to the way charity organizations do. Many schools and colleges get donations from alumni; they can also collect donations from other people so that all people have access to an education. As much as I support free enterprise, another possibility is that government can use taxpayer money to support education for those who cannot afford it. It is better if the money comes from private donations, but if schools are not able to collect enough donations to provide a free education to the poor, then government can help provide the rest. Ron Clark charge fees based on families' afford-ability to pay.

Now if we get an education for free now, what benefit is there to pay for it, even if it is a small amount? As much as we like free things, we put more value when we have to pay for something. The price of an education should not be more than most people can afford. However, paying something makes us put more effort to make sure we get what we pay for. Of course, even with public elementary education, we still pay through taxes. Those costs are just hidden.

Another option is that education should not just be limited to work in the classroom. Young students should be allowed to do apprenticeships and other jobs. Volunteer work at a hospital or charity organization should count for an education as long as it fulfills skill requirements. I have served in office positions for student organizations when I was in school. I learned more as a treasurer, president, and PR co-chairperson for student organizations than I ever learned in the classroom. These office positions teach leadership, communication, and organization skills that are used in most jobs and even in businesses. They teach critical-thinking, which is used in many jobs, instead of memorization, which is used in some but not most jobs.

Opening Doors or Closing Them?

Before World War 2, many Americans got married when they were 18. Although we may consider this very young, many of those people were ready for it. Back then, a high school education prepared them for a career. Now, it is rare to find anybody younger than mid-20s mature enough to get married. Basically, this means that we are getting less mature as a society. Shouldn't we try to improve or at least stay as mature as we were rather than become less mature. I am not advocating that we go back to marrying earlier, but we should go back to the maturity levels we once had.

School largely delays our maturity by delaying work and other real-life experiences. If we had the option to enter the work force early instead of go to school, we might actually be more mature than we are now. After all, our bodies are sexually mature in our teen years. As teenagers, we are biologically ready to have sex and make babies, so shouldn't our brains also be ready for that? I am not encouraging it, but our brains should at least mature as quickly as our hormones rather than slowly. Art classes are often the first to go when budgets are short, but they are actually more important than subjects like history and even science. Not only is art necessary in fields such as graphic design and interior design, but it teaches creative thinking. People who started websites like facebook demonstrated creative thinking in addition to technical skills. I read one yahoo article about a girl named Ashley Qayle who makes wallpaper for other people's blogs and websites. Ashley's website is called whateverlife.com. Ashly is a teenager and high school dropout, yet she makes millions of dollars through ad revenue. She made money by using technical knowledge in art and creative thinking. These are the skills that children need much more than memorization, which is rarely used in jobs outside of health care and other sciences. Of course, people do not have to use the computer to make a living in art. They can also sell paintings and other hand art. People can either sell their paintings directly or they can use their artwork for animation, advertisements, etc. In addition to visual arts, music and acting are also art forms that can be practical in careers. Music is important in advertising, entertainment, and the music industry. Although careers in acting are very competitive, acting classes can help people develop social skills and confidence necessary in job interviews and on the job. Why don't children have the option of going straight to art schools and other technical institutes at a younger age rather than being forced to go to public schools that teach many subjects that the student will never use?

Many people feel that school prepares you for a career. Well, that is true if you are a lawyer, doctor, technology major, or economist. However, for the average person, very little of what you learn in school helps you in your career. A salesperson, real estate agent, business owner, administrative assistant, project manager, or receptionist does not use his or her degree to find a job. Basic reading, writing, and math skills are very important, but what about everything else you learn afterwards? When I was in a job interview, I don't recall my boss asking me when Napoleon invaded Egypt or what the square root of 16 is. I don't remember having to do quadratic formulas or applying anything I learned in history classes for any of my jobs. Anatomy was a very useful class for me as a personal trainer, and I think it also benefits people who are not health or biology majors, but these classes should also discuss ways to keep yourself healthy and not just about memorizing how the human body works.

For most of history, very few people went to school. This is true even in wealthy countries like America. It wasn't until the 1800s that the US government made school mandatory. Why did they do this? Maybe they thought young children need an education to have the skills to survive the work force. Nope. That wasn't it. During the 1800s, America was going through the industrial revolution. Before this time, most Americans were farmers, and their children helped out with farm labor. Although farm labor was never easy, it was less dangerous than industrial labor. The government made a law that you have to be 16 years old or older to get a job. Now what happens when you have millions of children that no longer are allowed to work? They are idle. What happens to idle children? They might become criminals, so the government required that they go to school to keep them out of trouble. In other words, public school is a baby-sitting service for unemployed children.

Although it makes sense to keep children off the streets, there should be other options besides school. You should have the option to let your children volunteer at a hospital or other place. In fact, you should have the option to let your children get jobs. Most work is not as dangerous as it was during the industrial revolution. There would be no harm in letting children do jobs involve computers, bagging groceries, or other jobs that are free from major safety hazards.

There should be more freedom in the kinds of schools children can go to. Although you have the option to send your children to a private school, that's only if you can afford it. Even if you go to private school, your parents' tax money (and your tax money if you have a part-time job) is used to support these public schools even though you don't benefit from them. Some states have voucher programs to get a tax cut if you go to private school, but not all states have them. However, even with private schools, the government still controls the curriculum and accreditation requirements. Private schools just decide on the methods. With all these restrictions to your freedom, I am surprised public schools don't make you wear uniforms.

People also have the option to send their children to charter schools and magnet schools. However, to get accreditation, these schools still need to have a curriculum that the government decides. The curriculum we have is chosen partially because some skills such as math, reading, and writing are important. It is also important to have a balanced education. However, a large reason for requiring social sciences is to make Americans to be "good citizens." Although it is good to know about the civil rights movement, slavery, women's rights, and other freedom movements; we are also taught many things that are not true. American history and other social science classes are still very Euro-centric. They give the impression that Greece made many mathematical discoveries while ignore the contributions of India and China. They give the impression that Europe created the printing press even though China started the printing press 500 years earlier. Most Americans are Caucasian, so it makes sense for America to emphasize on talking about contributions of Caucasians. However, it is wrong to make a false statement that Europe discovered something when it was India, China, Egypt, or another country.

How We Can Make School More Practical

Schools should basically teach how they want, and parents should be free to pick which schools they want. However, I would like to give some ideas on how I think a practical school should run.

One thing that was beneficial to me in school was doing extra-curricular charity organizations. I got to hold office positions such as treasurer, vice president, president, PR chair person, etc. However, I would be able to learn even more by directly volunteering for the Red Cross instead of going to class volunteering for school club that works with the Red Cross.

Real estate courses are also very practical. Century 21 and other real estate firms have courses in real estate. Studying to be a real estate agent or simply studying material for the exam would be very helpful whether you want to a be a real estate agent, but it is also helpful if you want to buy or sell a house. It may be beneficial to be able to take such a course instead of most other school classes. We should have the freedom of taking such classes instead of going to school. Schools should still exit, but they should be optional. Schools should either be private organizations or nonprofit NGOs. Such schools would get money from school fees and/or donations. This way, schools would be forced to provide a practical education. If young people entered the work force instead of going to school, that would force many schools to improve their education to attract students and parents. Schools that do a bad job would go out of business, but at least students would have the option to go to the work force. Many schools that would go out of business include inner-city and other poor schools. You can argue that if such schools close down, that will mean more crime. I actually think if school is optional, that frees money to the economy. Which reduces poverty. In addition, people who chose to enter the work force instead of go to school have more money to donate to organizations such as Boys & Girls Club that actually prevent and reduce crime, something that school does not actually do. Trust me, forcing inner-city students to memorize boring facts will only keep them out of the trouble during school hours. However, providing them with activities can teach skills and cooperation.

I have sometimes complained about how schools teach subjects we don't use in our adulthood. I hear about charter schools and technical institutes that use innovative techniques to teach students things that are actually useful in careers. However, this idea of schools teaching practical skills in high school and even middle school is not new. For most of history, people who learned to read and write would usually enter trade school rather than learn more grammar and history. I say we bring back an old idea to a new age. After elementary school, kids should not learn as much about history, sociology, literature, and other things that will have very little to do with their careers. Instead, they should go to trade schools. Now these trade schools should be diverse so that people meet all kinds of friends rather than only spend time with people that have their same career interest. Also, a middle school student is usually not ready to know what career s/he wants. So trade schools should not be limited to one career field. They should have a broad range of classes, but these classes should be directly related to skills necessary in the work force.

So what kinds of classes should be taught in these trade schools? Computer classes would be essential. Our economy depends very much on computer skills. Such classes would teach things like Photoshop, Premiere (video editing), and other computer software. Maybe web design should also be taught. I would also highly recommend teaching students about different operation systems rather than just limit everything to Windows and Macintosh. Linux is a great operating system, but very few people know about it because it isn't highly marketed. Red Hat Linux offers certification classes; maybe they should start teaching such classes in high school. Art classes would be very important because they teach creativity rather than memorization. So instead of cutting the art programs, I would rather cut history, sociology, literature, and other classes that rely on memorization. Art classes can merge without computer classes.

Graphic design, video editing, and photo editing are all forms of art that also rely on computers.

The Apprentice: You're Hired

We often say that young children are too young to know what they want to do with their lives. Although I agree, I also realize that part of learning what you want to do for a career involves trying out a bunch of things before picking one. School right now is about studying a bunch of subjects and memorizing information for tests; it isn't about learning career skills. During the middle ages, apprentices were as young as 10, but most were young teenagers. Although many medieval practices were oppressive, I see nothing oppressive about apprenticeships as long as they don't involve hard labor, lack of sleep, or other forms of deprivation. In other words, I see nothing wrong with a 13 year old doing an apprenticeship in computers. I especially think that an 18 year old can do an apprenticeship in sales, real estate, and various other subjects. In modern times, we use the word internships instead of apprenticeships. Well, I think students in high school, and maybe even late middle school, should do internships. In fact, doing internships should be a requirement for picking a major...not the other way around.

Communication and debate classes are also important aspects of social studies. Whether you are in a job interview, having a job and want to sell your product, or if you are pitching a change in the business, you need good communication. Even managers, bosses, and owners need good communication. To convince so many people to obey them, people in high positions have to communicate well the idea that they are the bosses. After all, how else can one person control hundreds or even thousands of people? People in power do this by doing a good job communicating that one person can have more power than many.

I once said that we should not teach so much math and science in school because so few people actually use them. A friend of mine said that although only 1% of the people use such education, that 1% of the population is necessary for civilization to flourish. Now that I think about it, I highly agree. So I still think math and science should be a major part of trade schools. However, I think a few changes should be made so that the other 99% of the people can contribute to civilization in such classes. In math classes, teachers should also teach about bank accounts, savings accounts, how to use a checkbook, credit cards, etc. In anatomy class, we should learn about how to be healthy rather than just memorize the names of organs. In geology and geography, we should learn about things we can do to preserve the environment.

Study abroad is another thing largely ignored in schools. I regret that I have never went on a study abroad trip because I thought finishing my education would be more important to my career. The truth is, one trip to another country can help you learn more than 4 years of college. Well, it depends on what your degree is, but most people never use their degree. So for the majority of people, study abroad teaches more than college. Charity organizations such as CARE offer study abroad programs that also involve providing service. To learn more about CARE Corps, check out: http://www.care.org/getinvolved/volunteer/

Ron Clarke Academy is a nonprofit school that has study abroad, technology, and other more practical education. His website is http://www.ronclarkacademy.com/. Although there is a fee to attend, it is pretty generous. He bases it on income level, so if you make less money, he charges you less. If you make $30,000 and have one dependent child, it is $40 per month. That's roughly $500 per year to give a child a much better education than you normally would. That's a good investment.

Trade Schools: Taking Jobs Away from Adults?

One concern about making school more practical is that older people will not be able to compete because there is a large number of young people able to work for less or no money. These older people may not be able to attain the skills to compete. This is an understandable concern. To address this, schools can have provide continuing education classes to adults to expand their skills. These classes can be at night time, weekends, or other times that are convenient for people who already have jobs. For example, an adult who works in data entry might be at risk of losing his or her job to a student. (S)he can take a class on database management to improver her/his position in the company. Another option is taking a course on management, marketing, book-keeping, etc. (S)he can also take a class about video-editing or a course on getting certified as a personal trainer to find a different career. Such education can be supported by charging fees, collecting donations, or a combination of both.

Another option is for companies to have continuing education classes. A company can provide on-the-job training for its employees, or it can even provide classes for adults that do not work there.

Legal Studies

One thing that surprises me is that American public schools teach us very little about America law even though they are government run. It should be very important to learn the constitution in depth as well as know the laws of your state. Learning American law would be very helpful. Americans should learn about the constitution as well as the laws in their state.

Well-Rounded Education

Some people might say that school should not just be about training you for work but giving you a well-rounded education. I am not completely against having history and other social studies. I completely agree that education should be more than just career training. However, I don't see anything well-rounded about most schools as they are. The main focus of school is teaching how to memorize facts for a test. This isn't well-rounded. Most history classes aren't well-rounded. They mostly teach about war and politics. We hear very little about the history of medical advances, inventions, food, etc. You can get a much more well-rounded history lesson watching the history channel. You can learn about the history of things like cheese, automobiles. I have seen episodes that even talk about the history film. For example, I have seen an episode about the history of making the Star Wars films. It talks about Lucas' struggles to make the movie; he was even at risk of going out of business before the first Star Wars film. It made more money than he expected. The history of Mickey Mouse is also interesting. Very few people know that Mickey Mouse was unsuccessful before being made in sound. Also, he was a mischievous character, so Disney had to tone down his behavior to make audience accept him. These are not only interesting facts, but they also teach us the struggles of successful people.

Even geography classes need to do a better job of being well-rounded. These classes teach about the location of different states and countries. They may also have facts such as the income, imports, religion, language, population, and other features of a country. However, you really don't get to experience the dance, arts, food, and other parts of a culture. This would be a well-rounded education rather than just memorizing facts.

In addition to modifying education to provide more career-training, schools should also be a place to learn about how to make the world a better place to live. For example, instead of just teaching about history and political science, it is also a good idea to teach about different cultures. Students should be exposed to foreign food, foreign clothes, foreign dances, etc. I once took a class in high school called Model UN in which we pretend to be different UN ambassadors for different nations. Lastly, I think it is very important that we talk about current events and the news. We should also use these classes to raise awareness about problems in poor places like Uganda. Of course, raising awareness is not enough; we need action. Schools should also teach people how they can take action to help these areas. There should be study abroad trips that include relief and other volunteer work. Maybe classrooms should also be used to fund-raise for these causes.

Schools can provide information such as websites for organizations that help the poor. CARE is an organization that emphasizes on economic development in poor countries. One of their projects is providing micro loans to help poor people start businesses. This actually helps poor people get out of poverty. The website for CARE is http://www.care.org/. There are also other organizations that deal with economic development. Computers For Africa sends donations of used computers to villages in Africa; right now they are emphasizing on Uganda. The website for Computers For Africa is www.computers4africa.org. Maybe you never heard this about CARE or Computers For Africa. Maybe a friend told you. Maybe you read about it in a newspaper or a magazine. Regardless, I am almost sure you never heard about it in school. You might learn that Uganda is a poor country; you might even hear about Uganda's per capita income. You never hear about what you can do to help. The only way you will hear in school about how to help Uganda is if a student starts a student organization about it, but you will probably never hear about it in class.

Combining Subjects

Although grammar and other subjects are mostly useless after elementary school, they can be modified to be more practical. For example, I am publishing my book on a website called Lulu. Their website is http://www.lulu.com/. Maybe one assignment in a grammar class is to create your own book and publish it on lulu.com. The teacher can correct for grammar and other things, but telling children about Lulu can empower them.

Fun School

Having video games may be another way to improve schools. Of course, most video games would be useless in school, but many strategy games teach people very practical skills. Many strategy games are based on war, but there are games like Sim City, Monopoly Tycoon, and other strategy games that teach economic skills rather than war. I highly advocate these games.

In addition to mainstream strategy games, there are also computer games that teach people about global issues. One of these games is Food Force. You play as the UN World Food Program and have to distribute food to the needy as well as provide schools and other services. There is also games where you play as poor families struggling to get out of poverty. You have to decide who goes to school, who works, when to take rest during disease, etc. Such interactive games can be a great way to teach about global issues in addition to facts, figures, and movies. The website for such games is http://www.gamesforchange.org/.

One benefit to making school more hands-on is that it makes learning more fun. Oh my gosh...did I just say fun? How dare I suggest that school be fun? If students have fun in school, they will think they can have fun all of the time! Truth be told, there is some truth to this argument. School needs to be structured. Video games should be used sparingly. Having cultural dances and festivals can teach about culture in a fun way, but like video games, cultural activities should be used in moderation. I primarily recommend making school based on developing career skills. However, making it fun will definitely reduce the number of trouble-making students. If schools are more hands-on and sometimes fun, students will have less incentive to clown around and make trouble.

New Teachers

Classes such as economics and marketing should probably be taught by people who have careers rather than just by people with education degrees. Also, classes should be at actual work places as well as classrooms. Imagine if students can actually go to hospitals, office buildings, and other places to actually get hands-on learning. Although this happens during college internships, this should also happen in high school. Businesses can benefit by having students do internships at very young ages. Businesses can benefit by getting low-wage or free labor while students benefit by getting practical skills.

One thing we should probably let go of is having only full-time teachers in K-12. I still think we need full-time teachers for elementary schools. Basic math, reading, and writing are absolutely necessary. However, beyond elementary school, most of what people learn in the classroom is useless. In college, professors work full-time by doing research and teach part-time. Outside of research, classes are also taught by people with careers outside of education. Accounting classes are taught by actual accountants. Economics classes are taught by economists. Teachers in middle school and high school should be the same. They have full-time jobs and teach a few classes per week.

One big disadvantage of implementing my ideas is that many teachers will lose their jobs. They don't know how to play video games, so how can they teach them. They don't have experience in accounting, real estate, web design, graphic design, photoshop, and other practical career skills, so how can they teach them? Well, this is mean to say, but if teachers cannot keep up with the demands, then they just need to learn those skills. Millions of Americans are losing their jobs due to lay-offs, outsourcing, etc. If these people cannot keep-up, then they are out of a job. That's how it is. Why should teachers have it any different? I am not an advocate of ignoring the suffering of people without jobs. I want to help these people. There are charity organizations that help homeless people and refugees get jobs; maybe there should be charity organizations that should help people who lost their jobs to learn new skills and find new jobs. I definitely advocate helping people get jobs, but I do not advocate protecting a useless job just for the sake of avoiding unemployment.

I really have a soft spot for teachers because they work so hard. They teach school full-time, often to a group of students who are rude or misbehaved. They have to grade papers when they go home. However, as hard as they work, if there is no real demand for the service they provide, their job shouldn't be protected by the government. If IBM can't sell computers, it is probably because HP makes better computers (or more popular computers). Nobody should save IBM to make sure that their computers are sold. IBM just needs to learn to make better computers or be good at something else if they are to stay in business. Right now, IBM primarily makes servers and computer processors rather than computers themselves. So they learned to adjust to keep up with economic changes.

American factory workers lose jobs because they cannot work for lower wage and produce more than factory workers in China. They need to learn to be good at something else if they are to have a job. Likewise, if schools lose students because another school does a better job, then they just need to compete or get better at something else. Otherwise, they go out of business. This sounds harsh, but the rest of Americans will be a lot better off if schools compete and adapt quickly to change.

Now I am in the family business, so I am protected from lay-offs and other problems that many people suffer. So I do not understand the hardships that many people suffer. Nonetheless, if my family jewelry company goes out of business, then I will experience the same hardships. Although we will love it if people try to help us, we would never expect the government to give us handouts or guarantee us jobs. With all these people getting lay-offs, I truly support society helping needy people to find jobs. However, I do not support government protecting jobs.

Reteaching History

I am not advocating the removal of traditional subjects such as history and other social sciences. History can be a very useful class if taught correctly. It can teach us how we became the way we are, which may even give us an idea where we will go if we continue on the path we are on. For example, America was not always the economic and military superpower. Egypt, Rome, Babylon, Greece, Persia, England, and man other empires were on top at one point, but then fell. China has probably been on top for a longer period of time than any other country.

During the 1500s, China started to decline, while Europe started to rise. In the 1800s, Europe greatly surpassed China and even started the industrial revolution. China has now fallen way behind. When China was on top, it was because of innovation and hard work. China started to decline when the people of China became to used to their fortune and became lazy. Other empires probably feel in a similar way. Of course, there are multiple factors that lead to a fall in empire, but laziness is often one of the main reasons. Now America is number one. However, countries like India and China are catching up. Our economic growth is a lot smaller. Part of this is because the richer you are, the harder it is to get richer. However, there are other reasons. Americans do not work as hard as Chinese and Indians. We waste money on things we don't need much more than them. Chinese and Indians, on the other hand, are generally great at saving money. America is a nation full of debt. It isn't just loan debt and credit card debt. We even owe a lot of money to China and Saudi Arabia. Eventually, this huge debt will really take its toll. We should take a lesson from China's and not continue the same path.

History also teaches us about the civil rights movement, inventions, etc. It teaches the hardships that people faced to give us the comfortable lives we take for granted. It can motivate us to work hard to make our society better by bringing new ideas just as famous people in history once did.

Unfortunately, this is not the approach of most history classes. History is a class that I think is taught very poorly in schools. First of all, most schools just teach you to memorize dates of events. How important is it for me to know who shot Abraham Lincoln and whatyear it happened? Does it make my life or anybody else's life any better? I don't really care much about who shot Lincoln and when it happened because I can't do anything about it. I care about learning how NOT to get shot in this life. I want to know why people become criminals, how to prevent it, or at least how to avoid being a victim of crime.

In addition, we learn a lot about European and American history, but we don't learn much about the history of India, China, and Africa. Becauseof this, many Americans and Europeans may have an idea that Caucasians have always been ahead of the rest of the world. You hear about how Greeks contributed so much to math, but you don't hear about India's contributions. Our whole counting system of 1 to 10 came from India. You hear about Johannes Guttenberg starting the printing press in Europe during the late 1400s, but you don't hear about how the Chinese created a printing press 500 years earlier. Other than Egypt, you don't hear about Africa's ancient civilizations such as Nubia. This gives many people the impression that contributions to science and technology always came from Caucasians. Much of my historical knowledge comes from independent research. Why are we forced to study history in school, especially when much of what we learn in history class is biased and often not even true? I don't think learning history in school would be much better than learning it through independent research.

Your Choice

Now these are just my ideas of how a better educational system should run. However, under this system, schools would teach whatever they want, and parents would chose which schools to send their children to. So if my version of school is what parents want, the market would lean toward that. However, if parents prefer a school has a little bit less career-training and has more moral training, the market would lead schools toward that. If parents want their children attending a more religious education, then schools will be more religious. Maybe parents want yoga, meditation, and tai chi classes. Just as with other industries in the private sector, schools should be able to teach whatever they want while parents choose which schools they become "customers" for.

Of course, there should be certain limitations. A schools should not teach children to become child soldiers. It should not take advantage of children by having them work in sweet shops. It should not have orgies to teach them how to have sex. Of course, parents would not send their children to such a school. Even if they did, the government has a right to step in when people's rights are being violated; classes that force sex, violence, or exploitation are a violation of parents' and children's rights.

A school that doesn't satisfy the demands of parents risks going out of business. Parents care for their children's well-being. Even though some parents may want more yoga while other parents may want more study moral instruction, most parents will demand schools that teach skills that improve their children's careers. Politicians, however, are not concerned very much about children's education. They are more concerned with staying in power, and they need to cater to the interests of teachers unions. Keeping schools the way they are keeps teachers from losing their jobs, so this is a way to at least keep getting support from teachers.

A truly privatized schools system with schools competing would more or less create an education that prepares children for their careers better than a government run educational system. Schools would compete for business just like any other market. Competition improves performance.

Luckily there are school vouchers that allow parents to get a tax cut when putting their children in private schools. Unfortunately, not all states offer them. The economist Nobel Prize winning economist Milton Friedman talks about school vouchers. He has a website where you can learn more and even contribute:

http://www.friedmanfoundation.org/Welcome.do;jsessionid=286CC19 BEE21DA91531F93DC8A4539E7

English is Spelled Wrong

Since I am on the topic of school, I thought I would share my humorous views on English grammar. The English language contradicts itself. It is funny how schools teach us rules on grammer, and then they teach us to break those rules because of other rules. It's pretty funny if you think about it.

You would think that when somebody comes up with a language, they would try to make it as simple as possible. Since it is hard to memorize everything we say, we have written records to keep track of things. The people who came up with written languages were geniuses. A letter or symbol stands for a sound. When you put those symbols together, they create a word. Words combine to create sentences, sentences combine to become stories or other documents, and so forth. This was a brilliant idea up until somebody decided to create this language called English. Just like any other language, each symbol stands for a sound, and there are certain rules. The problem is that English always breaks its own rules. It's a miracle that English-writing societies can even function.

Let's take the word laugh. Based on the spelling, it should sound like "law-oog-huh." I don't see an F anywhere, so why does it sound like "laf?" In fact, why can't we just spell laf instead of laugh? Does it make life easier to spell it laugh? Would it offend somebody's beliefs by spelling it laf? Obviously not, so what's the point of spelling it that way? Now what about the word psychology? Shouldn't it be spelled sikolojee or sikoloje? Wait, now I'm confused. The letter I has 2 sounds. The letter I is in the word sick and bike. Well, wouldn't it be easier just to spell it sik instead of sick? So sikolojee would can be pronounced the same way we pronounce psychology or we can pronounce it like SICKology. Hmmm...that would actually fit. Psychologists do study sick people, so maybe we should start calling it sickology instead of psychology, but we should spell it sikoloje.

The letter C also has 2 sounds. It can sound like S or like K. So somebody might see sick and pronounce it sisk. Also, shouldn't bike be pronounced "bikee" based on the spelling? Sometimes people use the letter Y like in the work sky. So then, shouldn't we spell it byk instead of bike? But sometimes Y has a different sound like in the word yarn. So how is somebody who first learns English going to know how to pronounce yarn. Somebody might see Y in sky, so maybe that person will pronounce it iarn. But that sounds like iron. That's way too confusing. What's the point of having one letter have 2 sounds, and what's the point of having 2 different letters have the same sound? Why can't we just keep the rules the same? If there is a sound without a letter, then we should create one. For example, the word chat should sound like "su-hat' or "ku-hat." There is no symbol for the "ch" sound, so somebody thought it would be best to put 2 letters together to make one sound. The same is for the letter "th." The words "the" and "thumb" both have "th" in the beginning, but the sounds are different. They should have just made a new letter for each sound rather than combine 2 letters and make them have 2 different sounds. Somebody should have thought of that over a thousand years ago when creating English. Sanskrit has a different letter for every sound, and it has been around for 5000 years. Since English borrowed lots of words from Sanksrit such as guru, jungle (comes from jungal), cashew (comes from kaju), and yoga; you would think the guys who came up with English would have kept the idea that every sound has a different letter. Of course, that would make too much sense, wouldn't it? I have a theory why English has so many contradictions in its rules. Have you ever heard of a spelling bee? If not, a spelling bee is a contest to see who can spell words the best. Have you ever heard of a spelling bee in a country that doesn't speak English? I haven't. What would be the point of memorizing the spelling of words when each letter actually follows the same rules 100% of the time? My guess is that some genus decided to change the rules just so that we can have spelling bees. The spelling bee industry decided to change the rules just so they can stay in business. That's probably it. It's all politics. The guys who make the rules for spelling probably get commission from the spelling bee industry. It's probably a lot like how American businesses try to control Congress by donating funds.

Now that I think about it, who makes the rules for spelling. No seriously, I want to know. Is there a "Spelling Congress" or "Department of Grammar." In America, if you have an issue, you can write to Congress. I would like to write a letter to the spelling Congress so that they can change the rules to make things simple. Finding out who makes the rules is one thing, but how do they make these rules? Do they really have Congressional meetings to decide how to spell a certain word? Do they spend weeks arguing how a word should be spelled? Are there different parties competing with each other for election? I can see it now: "I think we should keep laugh spelled like it is. I'm a conservative." Then the opponent says" "No, we should spell it lauph." Ph also can make the f sound." I assume nobody would just make things simple and spell it laf.

Maybe I should just overthrow the guys who write grammar rules and make create new grammar government. I will put the laws into my own hands and be a grammar vigilante. I think a lot of people would support me. Many Americans already break these grammar rules when they write text messages and do on-line chat. People write "2moro" instead of "tomorrow." Now that's what I call a democracy, or maybe that is a grammatical anarchy.

Now you might say, "English has only 26 letters. How can we account for all of the sounds?" We can create new letters or even modify old ones. For example, the letter "o" has 2 sounds. For and top have two different sounds. In the word "for", we can spell it **fÖr**. In the letter word, "top," it can be spelled the same way it is usually spelled. The word "bore," can be spelled bØr. Other variations can include putting a line or apostrophe on top. This is common in languages such as Spanish. For the "ch" sound in chat, we might be able to use the letter "c." The letter "c" does not have any sound of it's own. It either has a "k" sound like in cat or "s" sound like in city. Instead, cat should be spelled kat and city should be spelled sitë. Chicken would be spelled cikin. Of course, this may confuse people who see the word cat and wonder if it is pronounced like chat or kat. So maybe we can spell chat as ¢at and chicken as ¢ikin. We can apply these rules to other letters.

It is a miracle that some words actually sound like they are spelled: Dog, hat, bit, hi, land, top, or, and; these words are spelled like they sound. That's the way all words should be.

Healthcare and Positive Medicine

Medical Fitness

The medical centers of the future will allow people to buy fresh food in cafeterias and also have a fitness center membership. What we currently call "health care" is really better called the sickness industry. This is ironic because the fitness and nutrition industries are completely indebted to the medical industry. We would not know about the effect of exercise and nutrition on the human body without medical research. Medical science created nutrition and fitness, and it should take the leading role in running fitness and nutrition programs. This is not only a more ethical approach, it is also a good business move. After all, if medical centers charge monthly membership fees for keeping people healthy, they will make more than if they charge money only when they treat people when they are sick.

This may sound like a utopian idea, but there are many medical fitness centers in the US. In fact, there is an organization called the Medical Fitness Association. Below is a link from their site that talks more about the organization:
http://www.medicalfitness.org/displaycommon.cfm?an=1#about

Positive Psychology

Although psychology is not a form of medicine, it is very much related to psychiatry and neuroscience. After all, it deals with the brain and mental health. Mainstream psychology focuses almost entirely on mental illness. Maybe now they should study happiness more. Now many people may wonder how mental health industry can make money off of happiness. After all, people go to mental health clinics when they have illnesses. They pay money for treatment and for taking pills that alter chemical imbalances in the brain. Well, remember that these patients only pay when they get sick. Most people do not have a mental illness. However, if you provide comedy, meditation, and other practices that increase happiness, both sick and healthy people will pay money for the service, and many will do so on a regular basis. That's how Deepak Chopra, a medical doctor, makes so much money.

Of course, Deepak Chopra's clients are very wealthy. It would be difficult for poor people to afford his services. My role model in medicine is Patch Adams. Some of you may have seen the movie "Patch Adams" with Robin Williams. What many people may not know is that Patch Adams is a realy person who is really trying to change medical care. Patch and his organization, the Gesundheit Institute, brings humor and entertainment to healthcare. In fact, his organization also goes around the world to spread laughter to orphanages, hospitals, and other with unfortunate children. The Gesundheit Institute has these"clown trips" in Russia, Peru, Romania, and many other poor countries. For more information on the Gesundheit Institute and ways that you can help, you can go to http://www.patchadams.org/. In fact, you can volunteer on clown trips that provide laughter to children in hospitals, orphanages, and other areas with suffering children.

Biotechnology and Wellness

Many people somehow think that improving health care involves using natural rather than artificial methods. Unfortunately, natural does not always mean healthy. After all, marijuana is all natural. Preventative medicine will emphasize on many natural remedies such as using fruits and vegetables more often then pills. However, the best medicine will also use artificial means when those have the best effect on health.

With the rise of biotechnology, people may use gene therapy and artificial organs to improve the quality of their lives. Artificial organs can replace damaged organs. Gene therapy can prevent diseases such as cancer, Leukemia, sickle cell anemia, and other genetic diseases by manipulating DNA structure to prevent the onset of these diseases. Genetic engineering can make foods more nutritionious by cross-breeding genes from one plant (e.g. Carrot) with genes of another (e.g. wheat) to make them more nutritious. For example, scientists can create wheat that is rich in vitamin C and vitamin A by cross-breeding it with carrot.

Although poor people might not be able to afford many types of biotechnology, it doesn't benefit the poor to prevent the rich from getting these benefits. Of course, maybe medical centers can set-up a charity to provide biotechnology for the poor. Also, biotechnology alone cannot guarantee good health. You still have to exercise and eat a nutritious diet; no amount of biotechnology will keep you healthy without a healthy lifestyle. Biotechnology can only enhance your health, but it cannot take the place of exercise, nutritious food, laughter, and other lifestyles.

Socialized Medicine: Good for Society?

Because I am talking about changing the heath care system, many people may wonder if I advocate some form of socialized medicine as in Europe. I totally support efforts to help people afford healthcare, but I do not believe in using taxpayer money to do that. The current health care industry in the US has problems, but having the government run medicine would be worse. When something is free, people might use it more than needed, and quality starts to suffer. So although medical care would be free in theory, the quality of care would be worse because patients would have lower expectations. They would not shop around for what they believe is the best medicine. They would just take whatever they can get. In response, doctors would not provide as good healthcare.

One thing that few people consider is that socialized medicine is not free. It is supported by tax payer income. So it has the illusion of feeling free and still costing you money.

Of course, saying that health care should stay privatized does not solve one big problem. How do you deal with high healthcare costs? I think the medical industry should still charge patients, but they should also try to raise money to support patients that cannot afford care. Children's Miracle Network is one well-known medical charity. Although children's hospitals are private companies that make a profit, many children's hospitals have non-profit charities to raise money for those who cannot afford it. You can learn more about Children's Miracle Network at http://www.childrensmiraclenetwork.org/.

American Cancer Society and March of Dimes are charities that raise money for medical research. So in addition to raising money for treatment, medical charities can also use funds for medical research.

We should also have a medical charity that collects money for health insurance. In fact, health insurance and access to exercise facilities should be part of a single payment package. For example, your membership at a medical fitness center should be part of the same bill as your health insurance. Funds from medical non-profits can help provide insurance for those who cannot afford it.

Having a widespread mix of profit/charity hospitals will not solve the problem, but it will be better than socialized medicine. With socialized medicine, you are forced to use your tax money to pay for care even if you don't think it is doing well. With a profit/charity hybrid model of health care, if people do not think a hospital is doing well, they have the choice not to fund it.

One option is for the government to create a charity fund for universal healthcare. UNICEF is a charity organization, but it is part of the United Nations, which is an international government organization. Actually, UNICEF gets 2/3 of its donations through governments and 1/3 of its donations through private donations. However, maybe a health care and health insurance charity should only rely on private donations.

Maybe the US government can have a health care organization withs funds collected through donations.

One advantage of having the government run a nonprofit charity fund is that funds would not need Congressional approval. The money would come from people who actually support the cause rather than from tax money. Congress might need to approve creation of the fund, but once it is approved, if people want to donate, they won't need Congressional approval. If tax money is used, it would be a very long process of negotiating and finding a compromise with the Democratic and Republican party, two parties that are at each other's throats.

Congress has a Democratic majority, so Obama doesn't actually need Republican approval. However, his health care bill will be much more successful if it gets bipartisan support than if it is only supported by Democrats. If only the Democrats support it, Obama will create many enemies. If funds come from voluntary donations, than it is less likely to cause political heat. Republicans have no problem with charity; they mainly are opposed to tax money being used for health care.

Although this health insurance charity organization would be part of the government, it would be best that the government hire people outside of government to actually run it. For example, the Federal Reserve is a government organization, but it is run by economists. Maybe this health insurance organization should be run by a combination of doctors, alternative health practitioners, medical charities such as Children's Miracle Network, and even some economists.

Business with a Heart

Redefining Capitalism

Many people associate capitalism with greed and immorality. Although capitalism is about accumulating wealth and private ownership, it doesn't have to be unethical. In fact, capitalism is usually more ethical than Communism and other economic practices. Capitalism is about the free market and making voluntary decisions, while Communism involves use of government force. Look at capitalism and look at Communism; capitalist countries have a much better human rights record.

Some people may consider European colonialism a form of spreading capitalism by force. Again, anything that involves using force goes against the principle of the free market. By definition, the free market requires voluntary exchange. European colonialism involved using weapons to spread business, which violates the principle of free market capitalism.

Part of the reason that people associate capitalism with immorality is that they may be confused about its meaning. For example, I had a friend say that America sends troops all over the world to maintain its empire because America is a capitalist nation. However, using military to defend business interests actually goes against the principles of capitalism. In a capitalist society, people privately own property, so using military force is considered a violation of property rights. Also, business transactions are voluntary in a capitalist society. Using the military for business transactions violates the principle of voluntary exchange. Slavery is also a violation of capitalism. It involves using force to make people work, and it involves violating another individual's freedom. When the military or any government entity gives any help to a business, this is not capitalism. Senator Ron Paul would call this "crony capitalism." I very much agree, By definition, capitalism requires economic decisions without force. When governments help big business thrive, this is also a violation of capitalism. Capitalism requires government to stay away from big corporations. Giving them special subsidies violates this principle. When government supports big business and uses military support to spread business, this is socialism.

Investing in Charity

Although charity itself involves giving something away, it doesn't necessarily require that the provider to lose something. Some charity organizations provide economic relief to many poor countries. As these people in poor countries become richer, they also benefit rich countries by being part of the global economy. Business and charity can both lead to a win-win situation and not just a win-lose or lose-win situations. A good charity should eventually make itself not needed. In other words, a good charity organization's goal is to make sure that the people it helps eventually do not need charity anymore. Likewise, a good business provides a service to the community and the world.

CARE is a great example of a charity organization that incorporates business. They have an amazing micro-loan program. They also teach farmers how to grow more food. Such principles help poor people escape poverty and even become successful. CARE's practices are beneficial to the world even if we wipe out poverty. Micro-loans can benefit small businesses, college students, etc. Farming is necessary to produce food whether people are rich or poor, so teaching people how to produce more food is always beneficial. For more information about CARE, you can checkout their website at www.careusa.org.

Bill Gates and his wife Melinda Gates started a foundation that donates billions of dollars to causes such as health care, education, financial services, agriculture, and other things. For more information about the Bill & Melinda Gates Foundation, you can check their site at http://www.gatesfoundation.org.

Computer Aid International supplies refurbished computers to third world countries. Although they only have a headquarters in England, they collect donations. Their website is at http://www.computeraid.org.

As important as technology are, the poorest people in the world need access to basic health care and other survival needs. Doctors Without Borders is a wonderful organization that provides medical care in these areas. They gave medical care in areas such as Sudan, Somalia, Congo, Ethiopia, and other areas experiencing war. Their website is at http://www.doctorswithoutborders.org/aboutus/. As far as food, disaster relief, and other basic needs, CARE and Red Cross are wonderful organizations to contribute to. Investing in basic needs is the first step to investing in the economy of poor countries. As these countries escape the cycle of poverty, the people will not only be happier but also contribute to the economy of the rest of the world. The United States, Japan, Western Europe, and other wealthy nations can do even more trade with countries that escape out of poverty.

Green Capitalism

Although most people look at capitalism and environmentalism as opposing concepts. You can argue that pollution is a violation of property rights. If a construction company builds roads or other things against the will of the people, this can be a violation of their property rights. Even if a government or company only does construction on its own property, if the construction causes pollution to other people, it can be a violation of their property or other rights. Economists call this a negative externality. However, it is very difficult to calculate the economic cost of pollution, and it is difficult to define property rights for things like air, ocean, etc. Some economists have ways to estimate this, though.

In his book, "The Undercover Economist," Tim Hartford states that we need to charge drivers for how much pollution they cause. Although people pay more money to buy fuel as they drive more, it isn't just driving itself that causes pollution. Driving in congested areas causes more pollution than driving in open areas. Hartford suggests adding a "congestion tax" or even have the private sector create a "congestion charge" for people who drive in those areas. He doesn't discuss exactly how this fee is collected, but he does mention that when London created the congestion charge, drivers started driving less in congestion areas. To add to the congestion charge, driver can be charged more during rush hour traffic, and less during the morning and other times when there is less traffic. In addition, during hotter time periods, more gasoline is used, so fees can be higher during summer or other hotter days and lower when temperature is colder.

Again, the author does not state how to actually find out when cars are driving in congested areas. However, I did a search, and it seems there is a machine called a "congestion charge payment device" that scans people's license plates, similar to police cameras that scan your license plate when you pass a read light. Just like the police mail you a citation when you pass a read light, the government or a company can mail you a bill when you drive through congested areas. Because roads are owned by the government, then the government would probably send the bill. However, I hope that in the future, the government sells roads to private companies so that roads become privately owned. This way, congestion charges would be truly a form of "green capitalism."

Many may argue that capitalism supports a person's right to smoke, but another person breathes that smoke without consent. From my point of view, capitalism suggest that the smokers violate the rights of non-smokers when they smoke in public places. So there would be nothing wrong with banning smoking in public places. Many restaurants have separate smoking and non-smoking sections. Maybe bars and clubs should do the same.

Finally, capitalism does not have to be limited to humans. Destruction of the environment may kill other living creatures. You could argue that although these animals and plants may not have legal private property rights, capitalism can still be used to support the right of other living creatures to live peacefully without the use of force. In other words, if you destroy a natural rain forest, you can argue that you are violating the territorial rights of other living creatures. You are violating the freedom of these animals to live in their homes. Of course, this is one way of looking at capitalism. There is no legal document supporting the private ownership of lands for plants and animals, so many people would not consider environmental destruction as a violation of capitalism. However, ownership and rights do not necessarily require legal documents. So this is a gray area in capitalism. There are multiple types of capitalism, so you can argue that this goes under the category of environmental capitalism.

Saving Green on Going Green

Many business are making huge changes to reduce their environmental foot print. Toyota and Honda are re-planting trees when they cut down trees to build factories. Walmart and the post office are buying solar panels for some of their locations. Most of us cannot afford to make changes as huge as these, but we can still make small changes that have a big impact. For example, most of us take down phone numbers, print out directions, right down notes, or do other things in business that do not need to be presented. We can easily reuse paper for such things. Now I am not suggesting that anybody reuse paper for presentations and anything that needs to be presented professionally. I am suggesting that we reuse paper to write information that does not need to be presented professionally. Not only is it beneficial for the planet and our health, but it also saves money.

In my family's jewelry business, we do a lot of reusing paper. In addition to taking down notes and phone numbers on used paper, we even reuse paper for our company's copy of invoices. Whenever we process on-line orders, we send a copy of the invoice to the customer, and we keep a copy for ourselves. We print out our copy on the back of used paper. As for the customer's copy, I use a clean sheet of paper rather than reusing paper. After all, the customer's copy has to be presentable. However, whenever I buy office paper, I purchase recycled paper.

Good, Clean Fun

Traditional economics does not look at the cost of pollution and other environmental problems. This is because it is hard to calculate. However, the cost is still there. While most associate capitalism with environmental destruction, taking care of the planet is actually in the best interest of the market in the long run. All business activities rely on natural resources, and when destroying natural resources, it is harder to do business. Also, pollution can cause cancer and other illnesses, which reduces productivity.

As consumers, we use the law of supply and demand to promote businesses that benefit the planet. We can even have fun in ways that conserve the environment. Most of us use Styrofoam or paper plates and cups for parties. If the get together is small, we can use silverware, ceramic, and other kitchen supplies. For large parties, we can buy leaf plates at www.verterra.com. These leaf plates are not only environmentally-friendly, but they also look and feel nice. If you are going to have a party, it might make the place look nicer with these kinds of plates.

For-Profit Charities

Many people look at charity and capitalism as opposing concepts. However, they can overlap. There are many forms of charity, but most involve helping the poor. Poverty is an economic situation. Helping people get out of poverty is basically about helping them make a profit. You can argue that capitalism is about making profit for yourself while charity is helping somebody else profit. However, capitalism is not only about individual profit. Large corporations have investors and stockholdrers. So many companies are about making a profit for share holders and not just any one individual. Brokerage firms help individuals get shares of companies. In a sense, a company with shareholders tries to increase profit for a community. That community only consist of shareholders of the company, but it is still a form of community profit rather than individual profit. We can extend this concept of shareholder profit and try to help people in poor countries also make a profit. This is what I like to call compassionate capitalism.

Although I support many nonprofit charities, I prefer the idea of profit for everybody. In other words, doing business in a way that provides job opportunity for the poor is the best form of charity. The key to for-profit charities is re-aligning the direction of profit. In other words, instead of helping the poor as a non-profit active but rather an effort to help the poor make a profit. Charitable donations are often necessary, but we should be working towards a win-win situation where everybody profits.

The pursuit of profit itself is not a problem. The problem is when a business works for profit at the expense of others. Although many people think that business by nature is driven to profit at others expense, that is not always the case. Toyota and Honda are working to build more fuel-efficient cars, and they are re-planting trees to replace the trees they had to cut down to build new factories.

Red Hat is an Linux-based company that combines profit motives and social welfare. Red Hat makes money off of the Red Hat Enterprise Linux operating system. Although they sell the desktop edition, they mostly sell servers. Red Hat also provides a free version of their operating system called Fedora. Fedora is also the operating system used in the laptops for the "One Laptop Per Child" program.

I have used Fedora Linux, and I like it much more that Windows or Macintosh. My favorite operating system, though, is Ubuntu Linux. Ubuntu Linux is provided for free by a South African company called Canonical. However, Canonical also makes a profit by selling servers. The owner of Canonical is a man named Michael Shuttleworth. Michael Shuttleworth made millions of dollars by running a security certificate company (i.e. secure servers or SSL); and he sold it to open Canonical. So the Linux operating system has shown how you can combine profit and social welfare.

Charity Plus Interest

Charity organizations should also consider having savings or other interest-yielding accounts. My family's jewelry business has a money market account set aside specifically for charity. Because it is a money market account, it generates interest, which means that we get slightly more from the account than we put into it. In other words, if we raise x amount of dollars for a charity, we get x plus a certain percentage interest, so that is extra money to donate to charity. Of course, the interest rate fluctuates over time. Sometimes it goes down, but sometimes it goes up. Either way, you get a rate of return.

Alternative Economics

I do not have a degree in business, especially not in economics. I am by no means an economist or a financial expert, so take my ideas with a grain of salt. Nonetheless, as somebody who is in the jewelry business, I have some insight into the principles of supply and demand that economists may not have. When we think of economics, we usually think of mathematical equations. The people who perform these equations are the experts. However, I would like to suggest an alternative view of economics. Economics is not about mathematical charts and curves but rather about ideas and psychology. When talking about how to fix the economy, we hear about the stock market and banks; we hear about where we should invest our money. Although such information is important, the true backbone of the economy is not the financial industry but rather businesses and creations. If you want to improve the economy, you can go ahead and invest in an IRA Roth and savings account, but you can do even more if you create a new idea.

Bill Gates revolutionized technology. How did he do it? By creating MS-DOS and Windows. How did Rosalind Franklin, James Watson, and Francis Crick revolutionize medicine? (Although James Watson and Francis Crick are given credit, Rosalind Franklin made great contributions, but sexism got in the way). How did Thomas Edison revolutionize electronics? He invented the light bulb and many other inventions. The creators of Facebook, the GPS, and other new ideas are the true experts on the economy. And the principles that they followed made the world a better place. We can use these principles to deal with global issues like poverty and environmental destruction. One way or the other, ending poverty and saving the earth will require dealing with the principles supply and demand. These principles need ideas and enterpreneurship rather than economic charts and equations to really spread change. Bill Gates and his wife Melinda took charge by creating a foundation that gives billion so dollars for charitable causes such as mosquito nets, computers in schools, etc.

Emerging Economies

India and China: Not the Threat We Thought

Even though America is falling back while India and China are rising, it is too soon to say whether any of those nations will surpass America. It is possible, but it can only happen if India and China learn to be innovative. Right now, their main advantages are that India can do information technology for cheaper while China can manufacture faster and for cheaper than America can. However, as India and China become richer, these advantages will diminish, so they need something else to reach America's level.

Many Americans are concerned about jobs being outsourced to India and China. While manufacturing jobs are being sent to China, service jobs in IT and call centers are being sent to India. While India and China are rising rabidly, the US economy is slowing down. Many Americans are worried that India and China will overtake the US. We never know the future, but India and China will never take over the US for two reasons. Most of the improvement in the economy of India and China come from jobs in American companies. The second reason is that India and China are contributing very few new ideas to the world but rather following what America has already brought to the world. American technology companies outsource IT jobs to India while many other American companies outsource manufacturing jobs to China. In both cases, India and China depend on American companies for their rise.

Although their are many people in both nations that start their own businesses, most of the growth is still linked to American companies. For example, Infosys is a computer company in India. Much of their revenue comes from the US because that is where much of the demand for their services come from. As for China, many of the products that Chinese factories produce are being sold to Americans. So India and China are very dependent on the US for these jobs. Unless they create more of their own businesses and depend less on the US, they will never surpass the US.

India and China also contribute very few new ideas to the world. The computer, Internet, cellphone, laptop, iPod, Blackberry, GPS, and other recent inventions all came from the US. India and China are not creating new products but rather reproducing or manufacturing products that America has already made. While Chinese factories often mass-produce American goods, Indian computer companies develop most of their software for an American market. Both nations contribute few if any new ideas to the world.

While India is growing rapidly, traditions and ancient customs still hold it back. Arranged marriage is still the norm in India, and women are still expected to be housewives rather than pursue a career. Women are still encouraged to perform well in school, but they are discouraged from using that education for a career. They are also more likely to be taken out of school.

Female infanticide, which is the abortion of female babies, is actually increasing rather than decreasing in India. As India's economy improves, and as Indian society becomes more educated, it seems likely that respect for women should improve. This is mainly because more Indians are getting access to technology that allows them to see the sex of the child. However, in America, most couples find out the sex of their child before birth infanticide is unheard. Technology alone cannot make India catch-up to or surpass America. India must learn to have more respect for women.

Corruption is also rampant in India. Criminals can bribe police officers to let them go free. Wealthy parents can bribe a school to accept them even if their grades are poor. Although the caste system is illegal in India, it is impossible for the Indian government to prevent everybody from practicing it. Most Indians live in a village, and the caste system impacts the lives of millions of people. Nearly 165 million Dalits, or members of the untouchable caste, faced discrimination in schools and other public places.

While India is a very traditional society, China is practically anti-tradition. Arranged marriage is unheard of in modern China. Children do not live with their parents after marriage. Most of society does not practice organized religion. However, China's Communist government still holds it back. Although China's economy is much freer than it was during the 1980s and earlier, the government still holds a tight control on many aspects of the economy. You can still be punished by law if you protest against the government or criticize the government in the media. The Chinese government still censors movies and Internet content with sex or other content that they do not agree with.

Although India and China are far from reaching the status of the US, life is improving in these nations. Women's right are improving. Political corruption is decreasing. Nonetheless, India and China still have much less freedom and opportunity than the US has. Until India and China let go of their traditional power structure, they will never surpass the US.

Of course, the rise of India and China does not have to bring America down. All three nations can grow together. Although competition is necessary, cooperation is much more important in our new global economy. India, China, and the US all trade with one another. The US provides jobs to India and China. China provides manufacturing to India and the US. India provides information technology services to China and the US. Indian and China watch America movies. Interestingly, Americans are now watching Chinese and American movies. India and China are now even watching each other's movies.

While India and China invent few things compared to the US, that may change over the next few decades. During the ancient times, India and China invented many things. Maps, the printing press, paper, the abacus, gunpowder, and many other inventions came from China. The base 10 number system was invented in India. During the middle ages, Indian and China were ahead of the rest of the world. During the 1500s, they got used to their success and thus became lazy. After the 1500s, India and China started declining. This is similar to the fall of Rome. Roman society became lazy from their success and fell as a result. During the 1500s, Europe regained the thirst for science and invention that Rome lost. While India and China were falling, Europe rose.

In the 1800s, Europe surpassed India and China as well as the rest of the world. This is a major reason that the Industrial Revolution started in Europe rather than India and China. America during the 1800s also had a great spirit for invention and discovery. Thomas Edison invented many things such as the light bulb and stove. Benjamin Franklin invented bi-focal lenses and the lightning rod. During the 1900s, America even surpassed Europe. America still creates many of the new ideas such as iPods, GPS for the public, etc. To come anywhere close to the US, India and China need to regain the creative spirit that they once lost that America now has.

Currently, China and India compete with the US for jobs. Jobs are outsourced to the US and China because they work harder and longer hours for less money. However, to truly grow, India and China need to bring new ideas to the world as they once did in the past. Once they do this, they can truly catch up to the US. However, once they catch up to the US, they do not need to push the US out of power. All three nations can become partners.

The Rich Get Richer, and the Poor Do To

You always hear that the rich get richer while the poor get poorer. Although this sometimes happens, in most cases, the rich and the poor get richer. Although this happens many times, the overall trend in the world is that the rich and poor get richer together. When the economy goes down, then the overall trend is that rich and poor gets poorer. The rich, poor, and middle-class are interconnected.

From the mid 1900s to today, the East Asian Tigers (Taiwan, Malaysia, and South Korea) grew from being about as poor as sub-Saharan Africa to being some of the most advanced societies in the world. The United States and Western Europe were also getting richer at the same time. While most people see the economy as a zero-sum gain in which one sides wins at the expense of the other, in reality, both sides can win.

While most people are aware of the rapid growth of India and China, very few people know about the improvements in Africa. Usually, we hear about AIDS, tribal warfare, starvation, and other tragedies in Africa. Although these things happen a lot in Africa, the living standards in Africa are rising quickly. Countries like Ghana and Nigeria are actually quite stable. Nigeria has a flourishing cell phone industry. South Africa has shown many improvements over the years. The era of apartheid has ended. Although many South African blacks are still poor, their living standards are improving fast. Schools are being built, and many schools are providing the children with computers. Michael Shuttleworth, a multi-millionaire computer tycoon, has a foundation that provides computers to poor people in South Africa. The Shuttleworth Foundation has a project called Tuxlab that emphasizes on computers for schools. This organization has done so well that it spun-off into a private company called Inkululeko Technologies. Now Inkululeko Technologies has taken over the Tuxlab project in addition to doing work to make a profit.

Rwanda is another African country that is benefiting from a growth in the IT sector. While most people know about the Rwandan genocide in 1994, very few people know that a new government is in power that is improving the lives of the people. The new government is spending government funds to develop fiber optical wires to allow Rwandans to access the Internet. They are also buying laptops from One Laptop Per Child and providing them to school children.

Latin America is another part of the world that we hear about poverty and violence but little positive things. Although there are still millions of poor people and victims of violence, Latin America is mostly improving. Brazil, Venezuela, and many other Latin American countries are doing quite well. Although many Central American countries like Uruguay and Honduras are suffering a lot of poverty, other countries such as Puerto Rico and Costa Rica have good living standards. Even the poor nations in this part of the world are still improving rather than gettin poorer.

Many people will assume that although poor countries are getting richer, the richer countries are going down. It is true that wealthy nations such as the United States of American and many European countries are suffering from increased unemployment and recessions. However, these are temporary lapses in the economy. The United States of American and most of Western Europe suffered a much worse recession during the Great Depression before World War 2. Europe was largely war-torn after World War 2. These were temporary episodes of economic fall. On the most part, the economies of both Western Europe and the US have been improving over the century. In fact, the economy on the most part is better than in previous decades.

Currently, the world is experiencing an economic crisis. So to a large extent, the rich and poor nations are declining together. Nonetheless, the long-term trend is that the world economy is improving. It is impossible to continue improving forever, so economic recessions and depression happen from time to time.

In the case of Europe, many European nations have socialist economies in which the government guarantees jobs to those with master's degrees. This reduces the incentive for people to work hard, which causes customer service and quality of goods to suffer. This harms the economy. Europe's high taxes to support its welfare state also damages the economy. America's falling economy is mainly caused by the mortgage and lending bubble. The economy was doing so well in the 1990s that many people took more loans than they normally wouldn't. The result is that many Americans have a large amount of debt that they can't pay back, which not only hurts borrowers but also hurts banks. This especially hurts people in real estate and those who have rental homes. When Americans have less income and more debt, they tend to buy or rent property less. The Federal Reserve lowers interest rates to protect the economy. This may help more Americans to be able to afford homes, which brings in money to banks that provide loans and also to those who sell or rent out property. However, this hurts people who having savings accounts. As the Federal Reserve lowers interest rates on loans, this also lowers the interest Americans get on their savings accounts.

Some Americans blame outsourcing for lost American jobs. Although many Americans are losing jobs when companies sends these jobs to Indian and China, this affects only a small percentage of Americans. The kinds of jobs being outsourced are mainly those in data entry, call centers, factory jobs, and other repetitive tasks. However, outsourcing also saves these companies money, which means more money for their already existing employees. Outsourcing jobs also reduces the price of products that companies sell, which means Americans can save more money. Because outsourcing jobs increases the living standards in poor countries, it means that people in these countries are more likely to buy American products, which means more money going into American businesses. As businesses make more money, they can afford to hire more American staff. In fact, they actually need more American staff to handle the increased demand of American goods. Even though many Americans lose jobs to outsourcing, outsourcing also creates jobs in the US as well as in other countries.

Of course, for those Americans who lose jobs due to outsourcing, it is hard to be optimistic. Their concerns are very important and need to be dealt with. Banning or putting limits on outsourcing jobs is not the answer. It may save some jobs, but it will hurt the economy overall. Job training or re-training is one way. Most Americans go to college and probably do nothing related to their degree. Instead, it is best to go to technical institutes such as Hi Tech, ITT, and other technical institutes that specialize in a specific field. Although many technical institutes have programs in information technology, which are often outsourced, they also offer programs in health care and criminal justice, which are unlikely to be outsourced. It is also a good idea for Americans to try and cash in on their talents. If you are skilled at cooking, making jewelry, or some other hobby, sell what you make. If you are skilled in fitness, you can become a personal trainer or other fitness instructor.

For parents that are worried for their children's future, I recommend encouraging them to get a job and gain skills now rather than wait till after college. Instead of emphasizing on a good education, emphasize on helping your children gain job skills and experience. Many high schoolers work at grocery stores, fast food restaurants, the mall, and other clerical jobs. With enough hard work, some of these high schoolers can get positions in management. It is also a good idea to encourage your children to gain experience in web design, Adobe Photoshop, software for making movies, and other computer software. Such skills can be very helpful in finding jobs, so encourage your children to emphasize on gaining these skills. Such skills are more important than good grades.

Obviously, there is no easy way save American jobs, but there are still steps we can take to reduce the burden of outsourcing and other economic changes. Of course, if you have not lost your job, it is likely that outsourcing is benefiting rather than hurting you. Despite recessions and other dips in the economy, we should be optimistic on the most part. We should be optimistic not just for America but also for the world. Even though terrorists are out there that want to destroy the world, the world is much safer than it was during earlier times such as World War 2. In the 21st century, it is unlikely that men like Adolf Hitler or Joseph Stalin will even hold such immense power.

Although men like Osama Bin Ladin have millions of fans, such terrorists have much less political power than Hiter and Stalin. In fact, it is unlikely that a terrorist will ever get such massive global political power. Even in oppressive countries like North Korea and Saudi Arabia, it is in the government's interest to limit their oppression mostly to their own country. These countries are unlikely to develop large empires and conquer several countries. They know it would lead to a huge war that would do them more harm than good. So rest assured, the world is a safer and happier place with a better economy than at any time in history.

Sources Cited

"Can the Cellphone End Global Poverty?" Sarah Corbett. New York Times.
http://mail.google.com/mail/?ui=2&view=js&name=js&ids=qk1v6dmi bzrk

"World Child Mortality at 'Historic Lows' Says Unicef." Anne Penketh. The Independent.
http://www.independent.co.uk/news/world/politics/world-child-mortality-at-historic-low-level-says-unicef-402317.html

Carol S Conrad. "Chronic Hunger and the Status of Women." The Hunger Project. June 2008.
http://www.thp.org/reports/indiawom.htm

"Prespectives from India." Tackling Corruption, Transforming Lives. United Nations.June 12, 2008.
http://www.undp.org.in/index.php?option=com_content&task=view&id=336&Itemid=0

UN Report Slams India for Caste Discrimation. CBS New. March 2, 2007.
http://www.cbc.ca/world/story/2007/03/02/india-dalits.html

Andreas Lorenz and Wieland Wagner "Red China, Inc: Does Communism Work After All?" February 7, 2007.
http://www.spiegel.de/international/spiegel/0,1518,465007,00.html

Survival of the Fittest: Healthy Living

It is important to have a good home and provide other needs. Most of us make a living from a job or business. If you do not have a job or business then your parents probably provide for you. Maybe you are a stay-at-home wife or husband. Either way, a business or job provides your living. Even people who hunt and gather or farm do some sort of work to make a living. For all of us, some kind of work is done to provide a living. If we are wealthy, we may give charity to provide a better standard of living for the poor. When we do charity, we are helping improve their standard of living. Whether we are receiving income or donating to help the poor, we are doing work to provide basic needs.

Although money, property, and other material things are important for our living, it is important to enjoy life and be healthy. In poor countries, people many people die of infectious diseases like malaria, tuberculosis, pneumonia, etc. In richer countries, people usually die of heart disease, cancer, and other chronic diseases. A healthy lifestyle can reduce the risk of these problems.

Charles Darwin is well-known for the phrase "survival of the fittest." For most of human history, humans were hunters and gatherers. They had to be strong and fast to survive. If not, they would die of disease, tribal warfare, or attacks from wild animals. Although humans no longer live as hunters and gatherers, Darwin's ideas still hold true today. Strong muscles and bones reduce orthopedic problems like osteoporosis and muscular dystrophy. A strong heart reduces your risk of heart disease. A healthy diet can reduce the risk of osteoporosis, heart disease, cancer, and other chronic diseases.

Exercise may not always be fun, but it can make your life more fun. If you go dancing, you will have more fun if you have more endurance rather than if you tire out easily. Of course, dancing itself is a great form of exercise. So if traditional exercises like running sound boring, try fun activities like dancing.

Types of Exercise

There are three important types of exercise

1) cardiovascular
2) resistance-training
3) stretching

Cardiovascular exercises mostly use the heart and lungs. Cardiovascular exercises include running, swimming, football, basketball, tennis, martial arts, and gymnastics. These activities reduce your risk of heart disease, lung cancer, diabetes, arthritis, osteoporosis, and even Alzheimer's disease by improve circulation of blood and oxygen.

Strength-training uses muscles against a force, although it also the nervous system and bones also assist the muscles. Your heart and lungs supply oxygen to the muscles during resistance training, but in most cases, you use less energy than when doing cardiovascular exercises. Strength-training usually involves lifting weights, but you can also use your own body weight like when you do push-ups. However, using your own body weight has its limits. You cannot develop strength with your own body weight as you can with lifting heavy weights. While cardiovascular exercises like running improve bone density, lifting weights strengthens bones and joints even more. Weightlifting is the best exercise to strengthen bones, tendons, and ligament; this reduces the risk of knee pain, back pain, and other injuries.

Although stretching may not prevent any diseases, it is a very essential aspect of health. Your muscles can become sore during both cardiovascular exercise and resistance-training. Stretching helps loosen your muscles up so that you recover more quickly. When you recover more quickly, that means you are able to do more exercise and get more health benefits. Of course, there is such a thing as too much exercise no matter how much you stretch, but that varies by individual.

Nonetheless, whatever your fitness level, you can usually improve it, and stretching can help reduce fatigue.

Aging Gracefully

Lower back pain, knee pain, osteoporosis, and arthritis are common in old age. However, old age doesn't have to be filled with pain. Most people who experience these problems in old age were physically inactive ever since their 20s and 30s. After decades of being physically inactive, their joints became weaker. There is a saying: if you don't use it, you lose it. If you go 20 to 30 years without using your muscles and joints, you lose control over them. Most people who stay physically active throughout their adulthood delay health problems associated with old age. Unfortunately, some people have a medical condition keeping them exercising. However, these people are in the minority. Most people who develop chronic health problems experience these issues after many years of being physically inactive. Of course, job stress and having a family take their toll on people's health, but I have met many people in their 40s and 50s who are in great shape, and they all are married with children. In fact, I know a 60 year old man in my fitness boot camp who is in great shape.

Healthy Eating

As important as exercise is, getting the proper fuel for your body is also essential. Your body needs carbohydrates and fat to provide energy and it needs protein to provide muscle. You also need vitamins and minerals such as iron, vitamin C, calcium, etc. This is not a book about nutrition, so I won't go into detail about what foods you should eat, but I can give some basics. Calcium and phosphorus help keep bones strong. Although milk is the most well-known source, you can also get calcium from green leafy vegetables and beans without getting the saturated fat and cholesterol of dairy milk. Beans and greens, as I like to call them, also have iron while dairy milk has virtually no iron. They also provide fiber and complex carbohydrates.

Meat, eggs, and dairy products provide complete proteins whereas soy is the only plant food that has a complete protein. A complete protein has all the essential amino acids while an incomplete protein has some but not all the amino acids. However, you can combine plant foods to get complete proteins. Beans and grains have complementary proteins, so if you consume both foods, you are getting all of your amino acids.

Vitamin A is important for eyesight. Carrots and mangoes are great sources. Liver is the best source. Vitamin C is important for immune function. Virtually all fruits and vegetables are good sources of vitamin C. Iron is important for oxygen flow. Red meat is the best source, but you can also get iron from eggs, beans, and green leafy vegetables.

There are many other vitamins, minerals, and other nutrients. Instead of going into detail about them, I will just give you a basic dietary guideline. Get lots of veggies, plenty of fruit, moderate amounts of beans, moderate amounts of nuts (especially walnuts that are rich in omega-3 fatty acids), lots of water, some flax seeds, and a daily multivitamin.

Wine: Good For the Heart?

Many enjoy drinking alcohol to relax. Medical studies also talk about how wine lowers your risk of heart disease. Wine has a substance called resveratrol, which lowers cholesterol. Other alcoholic beverages also lower cholesterol levels, but not to the same extent as wine. Lower cholesterol reduce your risk of heart disease, hypertension, and other cardiovascular problems. Because alcohol lowers your cholesterol, many studies suggest that alcohol also lowers your risk of heart disease. Many studies also show that people who moderately consume alcohol live longer than people who do not drink alcohol. This leads some to believe we should all drink alcohol for health benefits.

Although alcohol does in fact benefit the heart, it isn't necessarily the case that abstaining from alcohol increases your risk of heart problems. There are so many ways to lower your risk of heart disease. Exercise is the number one way to reduce the risk of heart disease. There are also many foods that lower heart disease as well. Grapes, which is were wine comes from, are also a good source of resveratrol. Whole grains, beans, and other foods high in fiber lower cholesterol levels as do chocolate and many other foods.

Many people know the excessive alcohol consumption damages your health, but even a little bit of alcohol can do some damage. For example, alcohol slows down your metabolism. A slower metabolism makes it harder to lose weight, and increased body fat increases your risk of heart disease. However, if you can keep your weight down, a slower metabolism can also lower your risk of heart disease. A lower metabolism means your body is generating less internal heat, which means it is experience less damage from oxygen molecules moving around. Nonetheless, since most Americans have trouble losing weight, a slower metabolism will make it even harder to battle obesity. A slow metabolism is only good if you can keep your weight down, but if you are obese, a slow metabolism keeps you obese, which increases your risk of heart disease.

The body considers alcohol a toxin, so consuming alcohol puts more work on the liver. Even though moderate consumption puts only a small amount of work on the liver, abstaining from alcohol doesn't put any extra work on the liver. Although a glass of wine may lower your risk of heart disease, if you replaced that wine with chocolate, grapes, whole grains, or beans, you get the cardiovascular benefits without the slower metabolism and workload on the liver.

Alcohol also breaks down calcium, which is necessary for bone development. I am not saying that drinking alcohol will necessarily cause osteoporosis, but your bones are healthier without alcohol. A little bit of alcohol every now and then is okay, but you can get the same benefits with other foods and beverages and without the side effects.

So if wine's health benefits can easily be replaced with grapes, chocolate, and other foods; why do moderate alcohol consumers live longer than those that abstain from alcohol? My guess is that since many people consume alcohol during social events, those who do not consume alcohol might be less socially active. People often frown on those who are different from them, so the social disapproval that alcohol drinkers put on those who abstain from alcohol can cause unhappiness, which definitely increases your risk of heart disease. There are many socially active people that abstain from alcohol, so it would be interesting to see how the results are when comparing socially active non-drinkers to socially active drinkers.

Alcohol increases your risk of oral, esophageal, breast, and other cancers. Even small amounts can damage cardiac muscle in some people. So despite the common saying that wine is good for your heart, you should also look at the other effects. Maybe it is the social interaction rather than alcohol itself that makes people live longer. Also, there are so many other ways besides wine to reduce your risk of heart disease.

Milk: It Does a Body Good?

There is a common misconception that dairy milk is necessary for healthy bones. Although milk has large amounts of both vitamin D and calcium, which few foods do, it is incorrect to say that milk is necessary or even the best nutritional source for developing bones. Although many studies support milk's benefits for the bones, the vast majority of these studies were funded by the dairy industry. In fact, other studies show that the nations with the highest rates of milk consumption have the highest rather than lowest rates of osteoporosis. The US and Scandinavia (i.e. Finland, Sweden, and Norway) have the highest rates of osteoporosis. Asian countries such as Japan and China have very low rates of dairy consumption, yet most people in those nations are lactose intolerant, or they consume very tiny amounts of dairy products. In African countries, most people consume dairy milk, but they consume a lot less than most Americans. Interestingly, Africans, despite being more malnouriched, have lower rates of osteoporosis than Americans. Dairy milk consumption does not actually cause osteoporosis. Nations that have high rates of osteoporosis tend to have high rates of obesity and low rates of physical activity. The US and Scandinavia have high rates of obesity while Africa and Asia have much lower rates of obesity.

Although milk is high in calcium, so many other foods are also high in calcium. Beans and green leafy vegetables have nearly the same amount of calcium as dairy milk. Of course, calcium consumption is not the only way to keep bones healthy. Exercise, especially weight-training, is the most important way to keep your bones strong. Consuming enough vitamin C, D, E, & K also maintain bone strength. In addition to the false claims that dairy milk is essential for health bones, consuming dairy products also have some health problems. Milk is high in saturated fat, which increases raises your cholesterol levels and increases your risk of heart disease. The milk protein casein may also increase your risk of heart disease, although the evidence for that is not strong. Even low fat or fat free milk still have lactose, which your body does not break down very well. 90% of Asians and 70 % of Africans are lactose intolerant. Only 15% of Caucasians experience lactose intolerances, so this is not as much a problem for them. However, for those who are not lactose intolerant, dairy milk has other health problems, even if fat free. According to the Harvard Nurses Study, women who consume dairy products regularly (i.e. 2-3 services per day) have higher rates of ovarian cancer. As for men, another Harvard study showed that men who drink 2-3 glasses of milk a day are twice as likely to develop prostate cancer than men who abstain from milk.

I am not suggesting that dairy milk is necessarily bad for your health, but I do not recommend daily consumption. I especially think the US RDA's recommendation of 2-3 servings a day is too much.

Laugh For Inner Peace

It is a lot of fun to laugh at something funny. You can laugh watching funny movies, watching stand-up comedy, seeing weird things happen, etc. Heck, bad things can happen, and you can turn it into something funny.

Laughing is more than just fun. It is good for your health. When you laugh, your brain produces endorphins, which are natural pain killers. Laughter also burns Calories. Laughter produces not only a feeling of joy but also pain-killing endorphins. Endorphins are chemically very similar to morphine. It is a combination of the words "endogenous morphine." However, unlike morphine, endorphins are beneficial for people's health. Morphine damages the brain and dulls the senses, but endorphins do not. Laughter also reduces your risk of heart disease and reduces stress hormones.

The Path of Laughter

Many people practice yoga or meditation for spiritual reasons or for relaxation. Meditation and yoga both help lower blood pressure and reduce mental stress. Laughter also does that same while also burning off extra Calories. However, while most people practice meditation and yoga as a discipline, people do not practice laughter. I would recommend that people try it. Many people have heard of laughter yoga, which involves laughing spontaneously for no reason. I do not recommend that. Instead, I recommend that people find humor in their every day life. People who meditate may do so for 30 minutes a day. Laughing everyday can also improve our health a lot. It will lower stress, burn Calories, lower blood pressure, and more. Many people meditate not just for the immediate effect of relaxation but also because it helps them deal with life when they are experiencing stress. Laughter can actually be a great way to manage stress because with laughter, we can actually find laughter at the thing that stresses us out. For example, at my family's jewelry store, we get a lot of customers who are rude and haggle to the death. Some customers even lie to try to get a discount or refund. Although this causes stress, we often later laugh about it.

Of course, not everything is worth laughing about. The death of a relative or loved one should not make you laugh. If you or somebody you are with has a major health problem, it is best to be cautious before making jokes. The movement involved in laughter can increase the pain in situations.

Laughter and World Peace

Laughter not only will help us improve the lives of your average individual, but it can also improve the lives of people who suffer from disease or poverty. Patch Adams, a medical doctor, has created an organization called the Gesundheit Institute that uses laughter as well as traditional medical care to treat patients. It also tries to humanize and de-institutionalize medicine. The Gesundheit not only provides care for patients in the US but also has laughter mission trips in third world countries. They provide their services free of charge, which can be a very good model for universal health care as opposed to the government spending precious tax dollars for universal health care and staying in debt.

For more information on how you can help, check out their website at http://patchadams.org/campaign/.

For information on his humanitarian "clown trips" check out the following link: http://www.patchadams.org/clown_trips

Love and Happiness

In addition to laughter, it is important to appreciate the people in our lives. Try to show your friends and family appreciation as much as possible. Thank people whenever you can. Shower people with appreciation when they do something nice. Don't just say thank you. Be very expressive in showing your appreciation. Of course, you should still tell your loved ones when they make mistakes. If you truly love them, you will not let their mistakes go but rather help them fix their mistakes so that they can improve. When they improve and do a good job, give them praise to show that the effort of improving is worth it. In fact, even when people are not doing you a favor, tell your friends and family how much you care for them. Make them feel very special.

Stress for Happiness

We categorize people into type A and type B personality. We call people type A if they are work-a-holic, have extremely high expectations, get angry easily, etc. We call people type B personalities if they are calm, balance work and leisure, and have balanced expectations. Most people say that it is better to have type B personalities than type A because type A personalities are more likely to have high blood pressure. However, both personality types have their advantages. While it is good to be happy with what you have, it is actually harmful to always be satisfied. Hard work and high expectations are the reason we have vaccines, computers, the GPS, and many other great inventions.

Of course, it is harmful to work so hard that you jeopardize human relationships. Your relationships with loved ones are the greatest thing that makes life worth living. Fun is important. Nonetheless, hard work provides the resources that allow us to have fun and spend time with loved ones. It is generally a good idea to be calm and control your temper, but it is also important to be firm and assertive as long as it is without being rude and disrespectful.

Sources Cited

"Exercise Associated with Reduced Risk of Dementia in Older Adults." National Institute on Aging. U.S. National Institutes of Health. JANUARY 16, 2006, 5:00 PM
http://www.nia.nih.gov/NewsAndEvents/PressReleases/PR20060116dementia.ht

"Exercising with osteoporosis: Stay Active the Safe Way" Sept. 22, 2006
http://www.mayoclinic.com/health/osteoporosis/HQ00643

"Exercise To Reduce Your Cancer Risks" 05 Feb 2007. Medical News Today.
http://www.medicalnewstoday.com/articles/62262.php

"Introduction to Exercise." Arthritis Foundation.
http://www.arthritis.org/exercise-intro.php

"SPH Study: Walking Reduces Diabetes Risk. (October 21, 1999). Harvard Gazetta Archives.
http://www.hno.harvard.edu/gazette/1999/10.21/diabetes.html

"Vitamins and Minerals." Health Check Systems.
http://www.healthchecksystems.com/vitamins.htm

"Vitamins and Minerals: What Do They Do." Netdoctor.
http://www.netdoctor.co.uk/health_advice/facts/vitamins_which.htm

Balch, Phyllis CNC. "The Disorders." Prescripton for Nutritional Healing. Avery. pp. 552 "Lung Cancer in American Women: Facts." National Lung Cancer Partnership.
http://www.nationallungcancerpartnership.org/page.cfm?l=factsWomen

"Will Wine Help Your Heart?" (1999). Hacsi Horvath.
http://www.cnn.com/HEALTH/heart/9907/06/wine.heart/

"Red Wine and Resveratrol: Good for the Heart?" (2007). Mayo Clinic.
http://www.mayoclinic.com/health/red-wine/HB00089

"Grape Juice: Same Heart Benefits As Wine?" (2007). Mayo Clinic. http://www.mayoclinic.com/health/food-and-nutrition/AN00576

Melissa Conrad Stoppler, MD. "Endorphins: Natural Pain and Stress Fighter." http://www.medicinenet.com/script/main/art.asp?articlekey=55001

Maud Purcell, LCSW, CEAP. (December 12, 2006). "The Healing Power of Humor." HTTP://PSYCHCENTRAL.COM/LIB/2006/THE-HEALING-POWER-OF-HUMOR/

Richard T. Penson, Rosamund A. Partridge, Pandora Rudd, Michael V. Seiden, Jill E. Nelson, Bruce A. Chabner, Thomas J. Lynch, Jr. (September 2005). "Laughter: The Best Medicine." The Oncologist. Vol. 10, No. 8, 651-660, http://theoncologist.alphamedpress.org/cgi/content/full/10/8/651

Rising in Love

In addition to exercise, healthy eating, and laughter, another important part of health is love. Love is found in friendships, but it usually starts from families. Although families include cousins, aunts, uncles, and other relationships; the base of a family is a mother, father, and children. Although I support gay and lesbian marriage, it is unfortunate that only a man and woman can produce a children together. I am glad that gays and lesbians adopt children, but to continue the population, a man and woman are needed. Although men can donate sperm to women, usually children are produced by sex. So a to some degree, sex between a man and woman is the root of all relationships. It creates families. Married couples don't try to have kids every time they have sex, and many people have sex before marriage. Some married couples are unable to have children for biological reasons, and a few married couples chose to get married but have no intention of having children. Some people stay virgins their whole lives. Even still, the majority of human families arise from some sort of sexual relationships. Marriage arose as an institution to regulate sex.

For thousands of years, societies developed marriage as a way to regulate romantic and sexual behavior. I do not believe sex before marriage is a sin, nor do I believe having sex with multiple partners is inherently immoral as long as they know about the other partners. But I do feel that there are negative consequences to a completely free sex life. There are many aspects to reaching to the point of marriage. To find a marriage partner, people in industrialized nations usually have boyfriends and girlfriends. People rarely go from friendship straight to marriage. Having a boyfriend or girlfriend is the transition phase. Americans refer to this process as dating. Some date many people before marriage while others chose to date a few. Some even date only one person and eventually marry that person. This is sometimes referred to as courtship. Others marry a partner who their parents chose, which is called arranged marriage.

In most societies, people marry only one person. Even though Muslim countries allow marrying multiple wives, most Muslims still practice monogamy. Only the elite rulers have multiple wives. Mohamed also states that you should only marry multiple wives if you can treat them all fairly. Since many people would show preference for one wife, Mohamed recommends most people only have one wife. There are some isolated societies in Tibet and India that practice polyandry, which is women marrying multiple husbands. This is uncommon because in most societies, there are more women than men. Also, a woman with multiple husbands may not know who the father is while a man with multiple wives can know who the mother is because she is the one who gives birth. However, it seems sexist to only allow men to have multiple spouses, so monogamy for both men and women seems to be the fairest marriage practice.

Although marriage is more likely to keep two lovers together, divorce is very common in the industrialized world. Many people mistakenly believe that America's divorce rate is 50%. This is false. However, the divorce rate is still very high. Nearly 30% of all marriages in America end-up in divorce. In Europe, divorces are also very common. It seems that the freedoms of the industrialized world make people also feel freer to dissolve their marriages.

Rural nations have much lower divorce rates. Many rural nations such as India have arranged marriages, so some people believe arranged marriages are more successful. However, lack of divorce does not automatically make a marriage successful. Infact, there are many unhappy arranged marriages. These marriages might not end in divorce, but this is because divorce is very difficult in countries like India. Society treats divorced people like criminals. Also, most women who get arranged marriages become house wives, so they depend on their husbands for financial support. The lower divorce rate in countries like India is not because of arranged marriage but because divorce is very difficult in those countries.

Backlash Against Working Women

Many people oppose the liberation of women. Although a small minority of people sincerely believes women are inferior to men, many people oppose women's liberation because of the high divorce rate.

Many people blame women for having full-time jobs rather than devoting themselves to their families. There may be some truth to this. Working women do not require a husband to support them, so they are more likely to leave their husbands than housewives are. Not only are they financially more capable of living without their husbands, but having more freedoms may cause them to have more expectations. In some cases, these women leave abusive husbands, but in other cases, they are leaving because they are unhappy.

Although many people would like to blame the divorce rate on working woman, both the man and woman are responsible for keeping a marriage stable. Many spouses get divorced because they have different viewpoints and fail to compromise. It is not always the woman who does this. It is often the man. In many cases, it is both sides who fail to understand their differences. If a husband and wife have disagreements about a major decision, keeping the woman from working does not solve the disagreement. It just puts her at the mercy of the husband. Most husbands are not abusive, but if one spouse is the only person making money, the other spouse usually has to follow the wishes of the spouse making money.

Even though women began working full-time in large numbers in the 1960s, the divorce rate declined in the 1980s even though women still worked full-time. Woman also started working full-time in the 1940s after their husbands went to World War 2, yet the divorce rate did not rise sharply until the 1960s. So working women cannot be blamed for the rise in divorce rates. One difference between the 1960s and 1940s is that the 1940s was still sexually conservative while the 1960s was sexually liberal. The late 1970s was the most sexually liberal period in US history, but the AIDS crisis caused many people to become more conservative. In the 1980s divorce rates went down, people became more sexually conservative, but women still stayed in the work force.

Despite any correlation between women entering the work force and the high divorce rate, other factors are actually the cause. During the 1960s, there were many changes in divorce laws. Divorce became much cheaper, and Congress introduced no-fault divorces. Before, you could only get a divorce by proving infidelity, abuse, or other bad behavior on the part of one or both spouses. However, in the 1960s, you could divorce regardless of whether any of the spouses misbehaved. Another interesting fact is that women's entrance into the work force and the divorce rate do not always correlate. Many people do not realize that the divorce rate actually went down when it peaked in 1980. The number of marriages that eventually lead to divorce peaked in 1980 and declined ever since.

In some cases, career women never marry because they cannot find a partner, or they choose not to have a husband because they want to remain free. When I say free, I do not mean to suggest that woman should do anything they want. They should not cheat on or abuse their husbands. However, they should be free to have career goals and have an active social life just like their husbands do. Many women are staying single because so many men are resistant to women's freedom. However, some women stay single because they are happy staying single. Many of these single women enjoy staying single. Oprah Winfrey is an example. There are also successful men that stay single. Sir Issac Newton and Ralph Nader are examples. However, it is hard to say if they are happier being single or just couldn't find a wife.

Divorce Rates: Lower Than you Think

Although you often hear that the divorce rate in the US is 50%, this is misleading. If 6 million people get married in one year, and 3 million people get divorced that same year, people assume the divorce rate is 50%. However, this is not so. The 3 million people who divorced were different people from the 6 million who got married. In fact, those 3 million people who got divorced may have been married in the 1990s or 1980s. Some of them may have gotten married in the 1970s or earlier. These days, fewer people are getting married, so it is possible that those 3 million people who are getting divorced now are getting divorced in a year in which marriage rates are down. Of course, all of these people who got divorced married in a different year. This, as well as other factors, makes it difficult to actually measure divorce rate. To measure divorce rate, you must look at all of the people who got married in a given year, and then keep a track of their entire marriage life until one or both spouses die. You have to look at these individuals and see if they get divorced at anytime in their marriage. This is very time-consuming, so many researchers estimate divorce rate by seeing who divorced within 5, 10, 15, or 20 years.

Another problem with divorce statistics is that it looks at total marriages and total divorces without adjusting for people who have multiple divorces. For example, if 3 million divorces occur in a given year, maybe 500,000 of those are from people who have been divorced in previous years. So people who get divorced 3 times, 4 times, or even more skew the data for everybody else, making it look like there are more couples getting divorced than the actual number.

So the divorce rate in America is more like 30%, not 50%. While many people say the divorce rate is rising, there is no data to back this up. In fact, the data shows that divorce rates are going down. Divorce rates peaked in the late 70s and early 80s at about 40%, and they went down since then. In fact, the divorce rates in the 1990s were lower than the 1980s, and the divorce rates of the early 21st century are lower than the divorce rates of the 1990s. With the global financial crisis. Divorce rates are falling further. We won't really know the divorce statistics for this decade until several years after 2010. I would imagine the divorce rate will probably be something like 25%. However, because society tends to always look for bad news rather than good news, people will still be saying that divorce rates are rising. After the financial crisis is over, maybe divorce rates will rise, but it will probably be something like 30% or 35%, not 50% or 60%.

Arranged Marriages vs. "Love" Marriages

In many nations that have arranged marriages, women are not allowed to have jobs, and their husbands are more abusive. In such cases, the women have no choice but to stay with their husbands. An abusive marriage that lasts is worse than a divorce. Even if the marriage is not abusive, the spouses often stay together because they have to. They mentally force themselves to love each other. It seems odd to have sex on the wedding night when you first meet. How do you have passion for somebody that you barely know? It seems more honest to naturally love somebody than love people because you are supposed to.

Of course, most arranged marriages are not abusive. In addition, love often increases in an arranged marriage. Although the wedding night must be awkward, the rest of the marriage can be different. Just as siblings learn to love each other naturally over time, so can an arranged couple. In fact, it seems that marriages in countries like India can sometimes be happier than marriages in the US. There are some benefits of an arranged marriage. Parents are less likely to pick a partner based on physical appearance and impulse because they are more aware of theresponsibilities of a marriage such as paying bills, compromise, sacrifice, etc.

However, not all youth pick partners based on hormonal impulses. Many people search for partners based on shared values. Moral values are a very strong foundation for a successful marriage. Although nations like India with arranged marriages have low divorce rates, there are many nations that have lower divorce rates than India but do not have arranged marriages.

Below is a list from the website "Maps of the World."

World Top 10 - Countries With Lowest Divorce Rate

Country	Divorce Rate Per 1000
Libya	0.24
Georgia	0.36
Mongolia	0.38
Armenia	0.42
Chile	0.42
Italy	0.47
Mexico	0.48
El Salvador	0.49
Macedonia	0.51
Turkey	0.51

Data from the link
http://www.mapsofworld.com/world-top-ten/countries-with-lowest-divorce-rate.html

Here is a table with divorce statistic from the International Monetary Fund. Although I often argue that government gives inefficient services, government statistics are very reliable.

Country	Divorce per 1,000
SriLanka	0.2
Brazil	0.3
Italy	0.3
Mexico	0.3
Chile	0.38
El Salvador	0.41
Japan	0.42
Ecuador	0.42
Thailand	0.58
Syria	0.65
Panama	0.68
China	0.79
Tunisia	0.82
Trinidad	1.21

Here are a few divorce statistics from Divorce Magazine:
http://www.divorcemag.com/statistics/statsWorld.shtml

Country	Divorces per 1,000 people
South Africa	0.73
China	0.7
Venezuela	0.7
Italy	0.5
Brazil	0.48
Jamaica	0.4
Turkey	0.38
El Salvador	0.3
Bosnia & Herzegovina	0.13

Below is another list of divorce rates from the website nation master. This table starts off with countries with higher divorce. http://www.nationmaster.com/graph/peo_div_rat-people-divorce-rate

Country	Divorces per 1,000 people
United States:	4.95
Puerto Rico:	4.47
Russia:	3.36
United Kingdom:	3.08
Denmark:	2.81
New Zealand:	2.63
Australia:	2.52
Canada:	2.46
Finland:	1.85
Barbados:	1.21
Guadeloupe:	1.18
Qatar:	0.97
Portugal:	0.88
Albania:	0.83
Tunisia:	0.82
Singapore:	0.8
China:	0.79
Greece:	0.76
Brunei:	0.72
Panama:	0.68
Syria:	0.65
Thailand:	0.58
Ecuador:	0.42
El Salvador:	0.41

Country	Divorces per 1,000 people
Chile:	0.38
Jamaica:	0.38
Mongolia:	0.37
Turkey:	0.37
Mexico:	0.33
Italy:	0.27
Brazil:	0.26
Sri Lanka:	0.15

Although different tables might have different numbers for the same country, it is likely that these data were taken during different years. However, the different tables still show that countries in Latin America, Asia, and North Africa have low divorce rates. Bosnia, Italy, and Greece; which are in Europe; have low divorce rates. India has a divorce rate of 1.1 per 1,000 people, which means many of these countries have a lower divorce rate than India despite the fact that they do not have arranged marriages.

My guess is that the strongest indicator of marital success is having a close-knit family. Joint families tend to have far fewer divorces than nuclear families, whether the marriages are arranged or not. In joint families, other relatives can intervene in problems, whereas in nuclear families, the spouses are alone to solve a problem and do not have a third-party to mediate. In addition, joint families are larger than nuclear families, so there are more things to do. Other relatives can distract or change the mood of spouses who are experiencing problems. Joint families also tend to be more close-knit. Having a close-knit family sets a precedent that family should stay together. This belief reduces the likelihood that a married couple with problems will get a divorce. Instead, they are more likely to work out the problems. The flaw with many non-arranged marriages is that people "fall in love." They start their relationship on an impulse, and then the passion declines. I prefer "rising in love." The relationship starts slow but gets stronger and stronger in time. Finally, Americans are used to so much freedom that they often feel they are entitled to get rid of anything that gets in the way of their happiness. They may view marital problems as stumbling blocks to happiness, so they feel divorce is the solution. Rather than taking responsibility for fixing the marriage, many people feel that they have a right to do whatever they want, so they divorce to find that happiness. Of course, there are many abusive marriages in which the spouse has every right to leave, but in most cases, divorces occur over petty arguments.

The Single Life

Most people in the world assume marriage is a duty instead of a privilege. Although I agree that most people are happier married than single, marriage is not for everybody. Nobody should be forced or pressured to marry. Some people chose to live a celibate life. Usually, these are monks and nuns, but I don't see why celibacy is only a choice for those who renounce careers and live in religious temples. Although they often serve humankind, so do many doctors, nurses, scientists, lawyers, soldiers, business people, nutritionists, etc. People who work in Red Cross and other relief organizations serve humankind. I don't see why they don't get the choice to abstain from marriage. The great pioneer of modern science Sir Isaac Newton, Henre' Dunant, founder of the International Red Cross, Clara Barton, founder of the American Red Cross, never married. President James Buchanan also never married. Ralph Nader, who is over seventy years old, and Condoleezza Rice, who is over fifty years old, have never married in their lives. Both of them are very successful people.

Some people say that married people live longer and healthier lives than unmarried people. When researchers conducted these studies, they put divorced people, widows, and lifelong singles in the same category. A divorcee or a widow is currently not married, so researchers counted them as unmarried. The never married are lumped into the same category as divorcees and young widows. Divorced people and young widows (those who become widows before their spouses become senior citizens) are not as healthy as currently married people, so they die sooner. Divorcees and widows make up a larger number of people than lifelong singles, so it is likely that the average lifespan of these three groups of people is shorter than the lifespan of couples who have been married for their entire lives. However, the average person who has never married is much happier and healthier than the average divorcee or young widow. However, to determine whether marriage increases health and lifespan, you have to look at each category separately (i.e. lifelong single, lifelong marriage, divorced, and widow).

The never married live longer than divorcees, demonstrating that it is better to stay single than to get married and then get divorced. Of course, widows and divorcees have been married at some time in their lives, so it makes sense to compare lifelong singles to anybody who has ever been married. The real question is not whether married people live longer than single people but rather whether the benefits of a lifelong marriage are worth the risk of divorce and early death of a spouse. Because nearly 30% of marriages in the US end in divorce, it seems that marriage is a huge gamble. This does not mean we should all stay single, but we should not get married because we assume a married life is happier than a single life. If we get married, we should get married because we truly love the person whom we want to marry. Of course, because divorce rates are so high, we should be cautious in picking a partner. As I stated earlier, we should take things slowly and enter relationships gradually, and we should see the relationship as a gift rather than take it for granted. Lastly, we should work out problems rather than run away from them. If you are not ready to take things slowly, appreciate your relationship regularly, and handle problems rather than avoid them, you should stay single. If you are willing to practice these things, and if you find the person you love, go ahead and get married.

Many people also get married to cure or prevent loneliness. This is not a good reason to get married. It is a good idea to have a strong network of friends. They can satisfy many emotional needs, and really good friends can also be there when you are in need. If you already have a close network of friends and find somebody you want to marry, go ahead and marry. However, make sure that you are not using that person to keep you from getting lonely. Make sure that you truly care for that person and are not getting married because you enjoy spending time with that person. Marriage can be fun, but it also has many headaches like paying bills, changing children's diapers, and other chores. Disagreements on these chores are one of the reasons why many people get divorced. Do not get married expecting lifelong bliss. There will be great times, and there will be hard times, so be prepared for the hard times, and make sure to have an agreement on how to deal with those times. Otherwise, it is best to stay single.

Of course, a marriage should not just be about work. Many people get married to have a partner for doing house chores and income. This is especially in arranged marriages. I have seen married couples who only talk about bills, house chores, and other tasks. Such couples are there for each other during bad times, but what happens when times are good? Although it is important to discuss these things, a married couple should also have fun. They should enjoy each other's company. A marriage based on fun only is a fantasy, but a marriage that is all work and no fun is miserable. You need both elements to have a successful marriage.

Some studies actually did research on people who are never married. They state that people who have never been married are more likely to die of heart disease, accidents, homicide, suicide, and infectious disease. In fact, they are five times as likely to die of infectious disease; twice as likely to die in accidents, homicides, or suicides; and 38 percent more likely to die of heart disease. Although lifelong singles are more likely to die of heart disease, this is usually because of social isolation. It is true that married people tend to have better social lives, but single people have active social lives usually do not die early of heart disease. In addition, the social isolation often happens because married people tend to stigmatize single people. When married people treat single people with more respect, there is less social isolation. It is also true that married people are less likely to die of accidents, homicide, and suicide. Because they do not have a spouse or children, single people are more likely to take risks. There is simple way to get around that. Whether you are single or married, do not take dangerous risks. Although single people are more likely to die of infectious disease, this is usually because many never married people have sex with people who have AIDS. In the US, couples get STD tests when getting married, so married people do not spread AIDS. There is a simple solution to avoid AIDS if you are not married. Never have sex, or if you have sex, make sure your partner takes and STD test that comes out negative.

At the other end of the spectrum, it is wrong to consider celibacy a virtue. There is nothing "pure" about being avoiding sex, nor is there anything dirty about having sex. In fact, if everybody stayed a lifelong virgin, life as we know it would end. Of course, that will never happen because most people have sex. Of course, because billions of people are having sex, there is no harm if a few million people decide to stay virgins. It is good that most people get married and have sex, but is also good that some people decide to remain virgins, and it might be better for the world if some more people did the same. Abusive people and those who get divorced would probably be better off staying single and celibate. I personally feel that people who are devoted to a career or cause, such as politicians, actors, doctors, and people devoted to charity may want to consider being single. Such people often work so much that it could harm a marriage. However, that is a choice that is up to them to make. Many people who work hard find a way to balance work and family. Actors in the US divorce very often, but actors in Indian and other parts of the world do not divorce as often. People should have the freedom to decide whether they want to have sex or remain virgins. The decision should not be done under pressure from parents, friends, religious figures, or anybody else. It is important to practice safe sex to avoid unwanted pregnancies and spreading diseases if you are not married. If you want to wait till marriage to have sex, that is also a good option. If you want to stay unmarried, that is another option that should be respected.

Sources Cited

David Zinczenko. (April 9, 2007). "Who Handles Break-Ups Better?" Yahoo News. *Men's Health.*
http://health.yahoo.com/experts/menlovesex/29235/who-handles-break-ups-better

Rose M. Kreider. "Number, Timing, and Duration of Marriages in 2001." *Household Economic Studies.* U.S. Census Bureau. p.13
http://www.census.gov/prod/2005pubs/p70-97.pdf

"Oprah Opens Up: "Why I Never Married or Had Kids" Michael Logan. *TV Guide.* October 4-10, 2003
http://www.venus-on-top.com/articles-Oprah-Winfrey.html

Daniel J. DeNoon. (Aug. 9, 2006). "Never-Married Penalty: Early Death? Study: Lifelong Singlehood More Risky Than Divorce,

Widowhood." WebMD.
http://www.cbsnews.com/stories/2006/08/09/health/webmd/main1880
465.shtml

John Cloud (Feb. 08, 2007). "Americans Love Marriage. But Why?"
Time Magazine "What's the Real Status of Divorce in America?" Legal
Zoom.
http://www.legalzoom.com/legal-articles//article13573.html

Misreporting on Divorce: Freakonomics Blog
http://freakonomics.blogs.nytimes.com/2008/03/21/misreporting-on-
divorce/

Be Fruitful and Multiply

The following chapter is strictly for humor and should not be taken seriously. I am not advocating any of the ideas in it; I am just trying to entertain you and improve your health through laughter.

Making Babies: More Ways Than One

Although humans and other animals reproduce by having sex, many creatures reproduce without having sex. Bacteria and other microorganisms divide in half. Plants grow by having water and soil provide nutrients to their seeds. Somewhere along the lines, some genius thought it would be a good idea to create something called sex. Sexual reproduction came as a way to combine genes to increase genetic diversity. This increases an organisms chance of survival as well as overall resistance to disease. On top of that (no pun intended), sex is fun. Humans and other animals enjoy having sex for its own sake and not just to reproduce. There is a common joke that the best recreation is procreation. Increased genetic diversity and fun while making babies...what more can you ask for?

Personally, I think whoever came up with the idea of sex to make babies was drunk. So many people have sex even when they do not want to have children. We have contraceptives now, but many people do not have access to them, and even Americans did not have the birth control pill until the 1960s. So for most of history, if you had sex, you probably had a kid. Millions and millions of unwanted babies were born because people acted on their sexual urges when they did not want kids. I have no problem with having sex as a way to enjoy your life. However, since asexual reproduction already existed, why not add sex as a form of pleasure but keep reproduction through nonsexual means. If two people kiss each other, they can satisfy their urges, but nobody gets pregnant. Two men having sex with each other or two women having sex with each other does not lead to pregnancy. In fact, oral sex between heterosexuals does not get people pregnant. If a woman sucks a man's penis, she will not get pregnant. If a man sucks a woman's breast, neck, or vagina, she still does not get pregnant. If a woman sucks a man's penis, she cannot get pregnant. Anal sex (i.e. penis in butt), does not lead to pregnancy either. It sounds gross, and I cannot imagine why somebody would want to do that, but that is another story. A man and a woman can be completely naked and all over each other, but if the penis does not go in the vagina, nobody gets pregnant.

Masturbation does not lead to pregnancy (unless you take the semen and put it in some woman's vagina). I think sexual intercourse between a man and woman should be the same. Although aheterosexual couple has the option of having only oral sex, it would be very difficult in practice to keep the penis out of the vagina during the heat of the moment. Male to female sexual intercourse should still exist as a way to satisfy hormonal urges just like oral sex, kissing, and homosexual sex, but it shouldnever, ever lead to having children. Instead, there needs to be another way.

Possible Ideas

One idea I suggest is that people be able to have children by the man sprouting a seed while the woman lays an egg. If the egg and seed combine, it turns into a fetus. The couple would have to feed it and water it just like they would a plant. Another possible idea is for woman to take a shit and the man to take a piss on the shit. After all, a man and a woman use the same organ to have sex as they doto take a leek. Okay, that's gross. Forget that idea. Another idea is to get an egg, break it, put it in a bowl, mix some other ingredients (e.g. egg, seed, semen), and put it in the microwave. After 5 minutes, you get instant baby. Of course, the first humans did not have microwave ovens. So some other method would be needed for the millions of years humans did not have microwave ovens. I guess humans and animals will have to improvise and stick to seeds/semen and eggs.

How Do We Change?

So I plan to write a petition to the clowns running the universe and asking them to change how we reproduce. Will anybody provide me some signatures? Maybe if I get at least 3 billion people to sign,

I could get things changed. Until now, I may just have to stick to celibacy. Hmmm, maybe I should stay celibate in protest. In addition to a petition, I might be able to stage a massive protest rally of celibates. Maybe I can unite humankind to protest by staying virgins for the rest of their lives until things change. If we all stay lifelong virgins, humankind will become extinct. Maybe I can get some other animals to join in. I tried that with a lions and monkeys, but they have mating seasons. They don't screw around all year long (pun intended), so they have only a limited number of babies. However, bonobos are pretty liberal. Maybe I can get them to join in. Since plants, bacteria, and other creatures already reproduce asexually, maybe they can support us. We will tell the bacteria that in exchange for support, we will stop making anti-biotics, although we will ask that they pick onsome other species. Actually, maybe they can spread disease to the clowns that run the universe.

The Universe: From Birth to Global Village

The Beginning

Billions of years ago, there was a huge explosion. This explosion was ultra-hot. In a few micro-seconds, this impact caused countless balls of matter and anti-matter to scatter everywhere. Things started cooling down, and these balls of matter and anti-matter collided together. This collision created pure energy. Since there were more balls of matter than anti-matter, there was still some matter left over, but the anti-matter was gone. Things started cooling down some more, although it was still almost 3 trillion degrees Celsius, and these balls of matter broke down into smaller pieces. The new balls are called electrons, neutrinos, photons, baryons, and quarks. These quarks joined into groups called protons and neutrons. The protons had a positive electric charge while the neutrons had no charge. A few minutes later, protons and neutrons joined forces with electrons to form a gas called hydrogen. Hydrogen was separated into groups called atoms. These atoms were made up of electrons, protons, neutrons, and a center called the nucleus. These hydrogen atoms had one electron spinning on the outside. Hydrogen atoms wanted 2 electrons on the outside, so they began sharing electrons with other hydrogen atoms. This created larger groups of atoms called stars. Stars are huge balls of mostly hydrogen. Over billions of years, these stars become old and ran out of protons. The stars cool down, making the outer layers of the star collapse together from the force of gravity. This collapse makes things heat-up again, causing the nucleus of different hydrogen atoms to fuse together. This created a new type of atom called helium, but there was still more hydrogen than helium. With both hydrogen and helium as a source of energy, the star began to get bigger to form a giant star. Over time, the intense heat starts cooling down. Because this heat was weak, it was red, so the star became a red giant. Although the outside of the star began cooling down, there was still a lot of heat left in the center. This heat caused helium nuclei to fuse together to form more new atoms: carbon, oxygen, nitrogen, and iron to name a few. This heat also created a giant cloud of dust and gas. This cloud began to cool down and compress into a new star called the sun. However, some of this dust and gas left the sun and mixed together with iron, created huge solid balls of matter called planets.

Birth of our planet

About 10 million years after the birth of the sun, rocks and gases fused together into a planet called Earth. The gases included hydrogen, carbon, methane, ammonia, water vapor, and nitrogen while the solids included iron, uranium, tungsten, sulfur, and other rocks. This mixture of gases and rocks formed a really hot liquidy metal substance called magma. Early Earth was a giant lava soup.

Over time, Earth cooled down, and some of the magma became solid rock. This magma was pushed down at the center of the Earth while the solid rock stayed on the outside, forming the Earth's crust. Water vapor escaped from these rocks to form clouds. The clouds cooled down even more and poured down rain. This rain formed our oceans.

Let There Be Life

After the oceans formed, nitrogen, carbon, hydrogen, oxygen, and other gases formed into a new type of atom called nucleic acids. Two of these nucleic acids are amino acids and RNA. Amino acids clumped together to form proteins. Eventually, another nucleic acid was formed called DNA. DNA, RNA, and proteins formed into a single unit. This unit grew larger by absorbing water and rocks. This unit later made copies of itself. These copies grew by eating rocks and drinking water. These copies made even more copies of themselves. We call this process of growing and reproducing life; these individual units are called organisms, or living creatures. The first living creatures were simple and small creatures called micro-organisms. Bacteria is one example of a micro-organism. Some others include viruses and algae.

The conditions of Earth, as usual, changed. In addition, some organisms got energy by eating other organisms in addition to eating rocks. To survive these changes, these organisms had to change, or evolve, their structure. Many of them formed into even more complex creatures. Some of these are plants and animals. Plants survived by taking in energy from the sun, just like algae, and absorbing micro-organisms in the soil. Animals consumed plants and other animals. Over time, animals evolved into more complex creatures to adapt to their changing environments. Fish evolved into reptiles and amphibians to adapt to life on land. Some of these creatures later became dinosaurs, while others evolved into small furry creatures called mammals. Some dinosaurs evolved into birds.

For hundreds of millions of years, dinosaurs ruled the Earth, but they eventually became extinct just like most other life on the planet. Mammals became the dominant creatures. Mammals were very different from most. The first mammals looked a lot like rats, but they later evolved into early humans, chimps, and other primates.

Birds and mammals had something unique from many other creatures. They had a part of the brain called the limbic system, which controls emotions. While most other species had to fend for themselves at birth, mammals take care of their babies with a lot of care. This deep sense of love is the greatest miracle that came from the universe.

Why Something rather than Nothing?

Many people want to know the reason why the universe exists and the purpose of our existence. The truth is, there is no purpose for the existence of anything. In fact, there really is no such thing as "the universe." Universe is just a word we use to describe all the things that exist in a single system. However, there really isn't a single system. Everything that exists obey a set of physical laws, but there is not one thing called the universe that contains everything. So rather than ask why does the universe exist, a better question to ask is why do matter and energy exist. The answer to that question is that there is no answer. Matter and energy just exist. Where did matter and energy come from? According to the law of conservation of matter and energy, matter and energy cannot be created or destroyed but changed from one form to the other. They cannot disappear, nor can they come from nowhere. Therefore, it is likely that matter and energy always existed. Most scientists say that the universe started with the Big Bang about 15 billion to 20 billion years ago. However, they are just referring to our current universe. Scientists do not deny that other universes existed before our current universe. So what we call the universe (i.e. the sun, 9 planets, the stars, etc), has been around for 15 billion years, matter and energy have been around before our universe.

The next question people ask is what is our purpose for existing. We exist because our parents had sex. It's as simple as that. Of course, in most cases, our parents wanted to have us. They wanted to have children to hold and love. This should be enough to make us happy. Although we are not born in this world for a purpose, we can find happiness in creating our own goals. Life is spontaneous and exciting.

Science and its Limits

Science has brought wonderful gifts to humankind such as the wheel, farming, telephones, computers, vaccines, the Internet, airplanes, etc. Science helps us learn about the world and the universe. Of course, science has its limits. For example, science also created nuclear and other weapons of mass destruction. Scientific views can also be incorrect and later corrected. Sir Isaac Newton's classical physics spoke about absolute space and time, but Einstein corrected our knowledge by showing that space and time are relative. In fact, motion is also relative. Of course, Einstein believed the laws of physics are perfectly predictable when he said, "God does not play with the dice," but quantum physics and chaos theory demonstrate that small changes in physical conditions can cause incredible, and sometimes unpredictable results. Cause and effect is not absolute. One event can cause one result, but in a slightly different situation, it can lead to a totally different result.

Most scientists believe that the universe began about 15-20 billion years ago with a big bang. Does this mean that nothing existed before the big bang? First, let's look at the definition of universe. Here is the Wikipedia definition:

The **Universe** is defined as everything that physically exists: the entirety of space and time, all forms of matter, energy, and momentum, and the physical laws and constants that govern them.

You can see a more detailed explanation at the wikipedia article on http://en.wikipedia.org/wiki/Universe.

Below is the Webster's Dictionary definition of universe:

Pronunciation: \□yü-nə-□vərs\ Function:*noun* Etymology:Middle English, from Latin *universum,* from neuter of *universus* entire, whole, from *uni-* + *versus* turned toward, from past participle of *vertere* to turn — more at worthDate:14th century

1: the whole body of things and phenomena observed or postulated : cosmos : as a: a systematic whole held to arise by and persist through the direct intervention of divine power b: the world of human experience c (1): the entire celestial cosmos
(2): milky way galaxy
(3): an aggregate of stars comparable to the Milky Way galaxy 2: a distinct field or province of thought or reality that forms a closed system or self-inclusive and independent organization 3: population
4: a set that contains all elements relevant to a particular discussion or problem5: a great number or quantity <a large enough *universe* of stocks...to choose from — G. B. Clairmont>

Basically, the universe by definition means everything that exists. The universe is not an actual thing. It is just a word we use to lump together Earth, the other planets, the sun, galaxies, space, time, etc. So according this definition, maybe "this" universe began 15-20 billion years ago. However, what does "this" universe mean? Because matter and energy are constantly changing, I think universe is really a meaningless word. According to the law of conservation of matter and energy, matter cannot be created or destroyed but only change from one form to the other. So according to this law, it is unlikely that the Big Bang was the origin of matter and energy.

Science also cannot explain what is morally right or wrong. Evolutionary psychology can tell us how we went from a tribe-centered morality to an becoming a global society. However, it cannot explain why we should be moral or why love is wonderful. The desire to spread our genes may have lead us to love our children. But it doesn't explain WHY we love our children or why we should take care of them. It doesn't explain why we love people outside of our biological family. Although we need to find a sexual partner outside the family to make children, evolutionary psychology doesn't explain why we have friends of the same gender. It doens't explain why people become gay or lesbian; homosexual relations cannot produce children, so there is no evolutionary advantage to it. Science is a great tool to allow us to help each other, but science can also be used for war. Let's use science to technology to make the world a better place.

World Peace and a Global Village

Although humans have been at war among each other for thousands of years, our groups are becoming larger and larger, which brings us closer and closer. We started as tribes, and then we became city-states. Now we are united as nations. Maybe one day we can unite as a planet. As the human brain evolved, we develop more and more advanced technology.

The computer is an invention that may have the greatest potential for bringing world peace. Computers can give you access to so much information. Whether you want to find a job, buy a product, or learn about your government, you can find it on the computer. Since we are exposed to so much information, we often learn about people who are different from us. Trade also helps brings different nations together. Although science and technology can be used to cause harm through creating weapons of mass destruction, it also can bring peace by providing opportunities and exposing people to other cultures.

Let us use technology for bringing peace. The heart of most wars are economic problems. Some nations go to war to escape poverty, while rich nations go to war with poor nations out of greed. Sometimes terrorists from poor countries attack rich nations out of jealousy or revenge. However, rich nations no longer attack other rich nations. If we can use science and technology to eliminate or decrease poverty, we may see the greatest evolution since the modern human brain. Some organizations send computers to poor countries. They include Computer Aid International (www.computeraid.org) and One Laptop Per Child (www.laptop.org).

Another organization is Inkululeko Technologies, which provides computers to poor children in South Africa. Inkululeko Technologies is a company that also has corporate philanthropy. Their website is at http://inkululeko.co.za/about/. You can go to the website of these organizations to find out how you can help. Computer Aid International takes used computers and sends them to poor nations. The other organizations take donations and use that money to buy new computers. Whether you have money or a computer to donate, you can make the world a better place by helping these organizations. The Universe arose and together from the cooperation of countless individual atoms. Now let us cooperate as individual citizens to bring out universal peace.

Sources Cited

(1931). Monthly Notices of the Royal Astronomical Society. 91: 483–490.

http://articles.adsabs.harvard.edu/cgi-bin/nph- iarticle_query 1931MNRAS..91..483L&data_type=PDF_HIGH&whole_pa per=YES&t ype=PRINTER&filetype=.pdf

Ivanchik, A. V.; A. Y. Potekhin and D. A. Varshalovich (1999). http://aa.springer.de/papers/9343002/2300439.pdf

"The Expanding Universe."
http://www.aip.org/history/cosmology/ideas/expanding.htm

"The Journey Continues."
http://www.aip.org/history/cosmology/ideas/journey.htm

Robert Shapiro. (February 12, 2007). "A Simpler Origin for Life." Scientific American.
http://www.sciam.com/article.cfm?id=a-simpler-origin-for-life

Global House

Earth, Our Home

Most of us feel that it is important to keep our homes clean. A dirty home attracts bugs and micro-organisms, which can damage our health. Also, clean homes are much nicer to look at while dirty homes are not fun to look at. Earth is our home and has similar principles. Lakes, forests, beaches, and Earth's other wonders are fun to see when Earth is clean. It looks bad when we see trash in beaches. It also damages our healthy when the air is polluted or when Earth is messy in other ways. Lung cancer and skin cancer rates increase from air pollution. We breathe polluted air, which damages our lungs, and the damaged ozone is not able to protect us from the sun's UV rays as well. However, most of us do not live as if Earth is our home.

Little Things to Save the Planet

Unfortunately, we depend on gasoline for fuel. We have to go to work, and we have the right to use our automobiles for fun. Buying hybrids can lower our impact on Earth. We can also carpool if we have a co-worker that lives near us. There are also other little things we can do. We can take Tupperware or other plastic containers to restaurants instead of using Styrofoam to-go boxes. Although plastic is made of petroleum, using a plastic container does less damage to the Earth than Styrofoam. We can wash and re-use plastic containers, but we throw away Styrofoam boxes. Styrofoam turns into poisonous gas over time. When we go to the grocery store, we can use canvas bags instead of plastic bags, which use petroleum.

Businesses such as Whole Foods sell products that are more environmentally friendly. For instance, many of their products are made from recycled paper, and some of their shaving cream is not made from CFC's. Of course, there are other grocery stores that are following this trend. I know Walgreens sells light bulbs that are more energy efficient. This is something else I think the radical environmentalists should take into consideration. Trees Atlanta is an organization that is dedicated to planting trees, and there are other charitable organizations that focus on environmental sustainability.

The nonprofit organization Water Aid helps people get access to clean water through filtration technologies. The website for them is http://www.wateraid.org/.

Many of us use styrofoam and paper plates and cups to eat food. While styrofoam turns into poisonous gas over time, paper involves cutting down trees. A company called Verterra created plates from leaves. They sell their leaf plates on-line at www.verterra.com. The plates not only are great for the environment, but they also look nice.

Going Green and Saving Green

Caring for Earth doesn't just have to be about our health. It can also be financially practical. Plastic bags come from petroleum. As petroleum supplies decrease, the price of gasoline increases. The more we use anything made of petroleum, the higher our gas prices. If we all use canvas bags in grocery stores, that can slow down the increase in gas prices even it won't eliminate the increase. Also, canvas bags are more durable, so they are less likely to break when carrying heavy items such as a gallon of milk. In some grocery stores, such as Whole Foods, you get a discount if you bring your own bag.

Tree-Huggers: Choking our Trees?

Environmentalism is a very strong movement in America. While most Americans probably think little about the environment, some Americans take steps to reduce their impact on the Earth. Such steps include recycling, carpooling, and other methods. A tiny but vocal minority, however, are more radical. There are some environmentalists who have protest rallies. One group of environmentalists, called tree huggers, camp in forests and refuse to move from them to prevent business from developing in that area. In San Francisco, a group of tree-huggers is protesting the development of a sports stadium. Although this is well meaning, it will not do anything to improve the environment. All it will do is delay development of the stadium but give environmentalism a bad name.

We all should take steps to preserve planet Earth. It provides food and water to living creatures. Earth also provides us with mountains, forests, oceans, and other beautiful sights. However, radical environmentalism is not the answer. We cannot stop development of stadiums and other facilities. For one thing, it is hypocritical. People had to cut down trees to build our homes. The tree huggers who protest loudly would not have homes without people cutting down trees. They also went to school and have jobs in areas that once had trees. These trees were cut down to design schools, offices, and other buildings. Maybe we should have protested the building of these homes, schools, and offices. Perhaps we should all live in the forest. This way, trees would never have to be cut down. I agree with saving trees, but we cannot protest any new development that destroys trees. Replanting trees is a better option that will get more support. If you make the environmental movement seem to extremist, you won't get any support from businesses; that will lead to more environmental damage than being more moderate, which gets you some support from businesses.

Sustainable Development

Of course, the environmental movement raises important issues. Even though development is important, it also causes damage to our environment. We need to find ways to develop while also minimizing damage to Earth. So how can we do that? In the case of trees, we can work with businesses to help them plant new trees after cutting down trees for business purposes. Toyota is an automobile giant; they have to build new factories and plants as their business grows. However, after cutting down trees to build these business centers, Toyota replants trees in a nearby area. Toyota also uses solar panels to supply electricity in many of their factories. Obviously, Toyota does damage to the environment, but they are also replenishing the Earth by planting new trees and using alternative energy sources. Toyota is also building hybrid cars and doing research on alternative fuel sources to reduce their dependence on oil. Tree huggers should work with businesses to follow the example of Toyota and replant trees after building the stadium and other facilities. Businesses are more receptive to these tactics. However, protests just leave a sour taste in the mouth of businesses and the public. In the long run, tree hugging damages the environment by making concern for the Earth seem like a self-righteous path of self-denial. If we really care about planet Earth, we should take gradual steps that can still allow people to enjoy their lives while letting businesses continue to grow. This will win over businesses and the public to environmental conservation.

Global Community

Different cultures have their own views about family and friendship. Although there are a variety of ways in how people deal with relationships, most are divided into four possible categories:

1. individualistic
2. collectivist
3. conservative
4. liberal

There can be overlap in the different categories. For example, collectivist societies tend to be conservative while individualistic societies tend to be liberal. Also, most societies have at least a little bit of all the categories. Now let me go more into detail about the meaning of these categories.

Individualism is about an individual's right to make his or her decision. Collectivism is about the importance of working together as a group and following group rules. America is often considered an individualistic society. When Americans become adults, it is believed that they can do whatever career they want, marry whoever they want, and make other choices. Many European countries are also considered individualistic. Africa, the Middle East, and India are considered collectivist societies. Even adults in these cultures often need approval to make many decisions. In some cases, these people work in a family farm or family business, but this is not always the case. Arranged marriages are also common in these cultures, but this is not always the case. However, even when picking a husband or wife by choice, people in these cultures are expected to get approval from parents and society to marry.

Conservatism is about preserving traditional values. Usually conservatives are against gay marriage and sex before marriage. They consider it immoral to watch pornography. In many cases, conservatism suggests that parents have authority over children and men have authority over women. In some conservative societies, women are expected to stay at home while the husbands work. Liberalism is about individual choices. Liberals often support sex before marriage and usually support abortion rights. Many also support gay marriage.

Generally conservative societies stress the importance of marriage. Liberals may also consider marriage very important, but they are more likely to support a person staying unmarried even at the age of 30 or 40. Of course, most liberals get married, but conservatives usually expect marriage at an earlier age. The exception is that conservatives may support a life without marriage if a man wants to be a monk or woman becomes a nun. Liberals, on the other hand, are more willing to support a person staying single even without religious reasons. Most liberals are religious, but conservatives are generally more religious.

Although individualistic and liberal societies generally have more freedom, there are some positive aspects of a collectivism and conservatism society. In collectivist societies, families tend to be closer. Villages and neighborhoods also tend to be closer in collectivist societies. There is more social support during natural disasters, marriage problems, and other situations. In individualistic and liberal societies, people may have to deal with their problems by themselves.

Divorce rates tend to be much lower in conservative societies. In some cases, this is because an abused woman can leave her husband in a liberal society, while conservative societies often look down on divorce even in these cases. However, this is not always the case. In many cases, liberal people might divorce because they "fell out of love" while conservative people believe in sticking together during hard times. Of course, there are liberals who stay together and conservatives who divorce, but generally conservatives divorce less often.

Although collectivist societies tend to have closer families and neighborhoods, individualistic societies tend to have more tolerance for different races, religions, and other groups. For example, a village in India may have a closer social bond than a neighborhood in the US. They also provide better hospitality. However, this is usually as long as the people in the village are the same race, religion, etc. The Indian village may have more religious conflict that may even lead to violence while the American neighborhood may have people of different cultures that get along well. If the person from the Indian village wants to marry somebody African or Chinese, they may be punished or kicked out. In the American neighborhood, this is less often the case.

Collectivist societies are more likely to have respect for elders. In many of these societies, children take care of their parents in old age. In India, sons often live with and take care of their parents when they get old. This is often true in Africa, the Middle East, and many East Asian societies like Okinawa. This is sometimes the case in America but pretty uncommon. In China, children usually do not live with parents after marriage, but they usually live very close.

Societies that are individualistic and liberal still have many collectivist and conservative practices. For example, most Americans may have sex before marriage, but most still oppose gay marriage. Most Americans are still religious, and many look down on atheists and other nonreligious people. Most Americans still follow rules and laws. Even though women have equal freedom by American law, men still hold much more power than women. America still has never had a female president. There are some female CEOs, but much less than men. Maybe this is because of discrimination, but maybe this is because women are not as hungry for power as men. Maybe both are true. Either way, this still shows a conservative approach to the status of men and women. This is often the case in Europe also.

Even in liberal societies, most people believe in marrying only one person at a time. Just like conservative societies, liberal societies give women a harder time if she has relations with multiple men, and they are more forgiving of men who have relationships with multiple women. A liberal society will not stone a woman to death for extra-marital relations as in many Middle Eastern countries, but liberal societies still look down on extra-marital relations, and they still have higher expectations on women to be faithful and have lower expectations for men. So liberal societies can still have conservative elements. Likewise, there are conservatives who still practice liberal behavior. In America, most conservatives are devout Christians. Conservative Christians in America usually support a women's right to get a job. Most American conservatives do not take care of their parents in old age like conservatives in other countries.

Being born in America and having parents from India, I often see the benefit in combining these different social behaviors. I strongly support individual freedom to marry who you want, get whatever job or start whatever business as you want as long as it doesn't harm anybody. However, I still believe that many liberal societies divorce too quickly. I support divorce if there is abuse in the relationship, but I am against divorce just because a couple argues. A marriage isn't bad just because the couple argues. Conflict happens in all marriages. I also believe it is important to take care of parents in old age. It isn't necessary to live with your parents during their old age, especially if you have a job that is far away. If you have a job near your parents, you have the choice to live with them, but if you don't live with them, it is a good idea to check up on them and take care of them when you can (e.g. weekends).

In cases that children decide to live with parents after marriage, it is not necessary that the wife always lives with the husband's parents. The husband can be open to moving in with his wife and her parents, or they can live with both parents. They can either go back and forth or all live under one roof.

I also support an individual's freedom to stay unmarried. Just because somebody is 30 or 40 years old doesn't mean that he or she has to get married. Overall, I am against arranged marriage, but if somebody honestly agrees to an arranged marriage, we should respect his or her decision.

Sources Cited

Bronwen Humphries (1994)
"The Diet of Early Humans: What did our ancestors eat?"
http://www.ivu.org/history/early/ancestors.html

Australopithecines
http://www.stanford.edu/~harryg/protected/chp18.htm

Consciousness

What Causes Consciousness?

Being conscious is an amazing thing. How is it that we are able to see, hear, smell, taste, and feel? Where did these abilities come from? Why is it that humans and other animals have these abilities, but a rock does not? There really is no satisfying answer to this question. One answer is that humans and other animals have brains while rocks do not. Of course, plants are living creatures, and they do not have brains. Plants do not have a nervous system, but they have hormones. In addition to plants, there are other living creatures without a brain such as algae, bacteria, viruses, fungi, etc. Some people might consider that these living creatures also have consciousness. However, even among this minority, consciousness is limited to living creatures.

Now why might consciousness be in living creatures but not in nonliving objects. Is there some spirit that enters the brain? If living creatures without brains have consciousness, what do they share with animals? Well, all living creatures have DNA and cells, even if they do not have brains. Why does a spirit enter cells but not enter water, a rock, dirt, or some other nonliving object?

Regardless of whether consciousness is only in animals, in all living creatures, or even in some nonliving objects such as rocks; there is no single thing that leads to consciousness. Even if spirits and souls exist, they alone cannot fully explain consciousness. Consciousness is a complex network of interactions in the brain, heart, hormones, DNA, and other parts of a living creature.

I do not know a lot about the anatomy of plants and micro-organisms, so I will limit my discussion to explaining animal anatomy. All animals have a brain. The brain connects to the rest of the body through nerves. Nerves are like wires. They send signals from the brain to the rest of the body and also send signals from the rest of the body to the brain. These signals create our senses. When signals go from your hand to your brain, this creates the sensation of touch. Your hand tells your brain what it is touching and how it feels while the brain tells your hand how to respond. If you touch something hot, your brain tells your hand to move.

Thinking and Feeling

Your body isn't the only thing that communicates with your brain. Your thoughts and emotions send signals to your brain. Although you cannot directly control your emotions, you can control your thoughts, which can sometimes change your emotions. The actions and words of people around you affect your thoughts. Events in your life also affect your thoughts. You do not have total control of how you react to them, but you have some control. Your thoughts affect the behavior of your brain. When you are happy, your brain releases different hormones depending on what type of happiness you have. If you are exercising or laughing, your body releases endorphins, which are natural pain killers that are chemically very similar to morphine. When you are in love, your body releases oxytocin and sometimes dopamine. Your brain is more likely to release oxytocin when you have a long-term loving bond with somebody while it usually releases more dopamine when you are physically or sexually attracted to somebody. It is however, possible to have a long-term, loving relationship with somebody that you are also sexually attracted to. So you can release both oxytocin and dopamine if you are in a lifelong marriage with a spouse you are also highly attracted to.

Mothers release oxytocin when they are giving milk to babies. When you are excited, your brain releases epinephrine, also known as adrenaline, and norepinephrine. Interestingly, your brain releases epinephrine and norepinephrine when you are scared or nervous. It also releases cortisol when you experience fear. Epinephrine, norepinephrine, and epinephrine are called adrenal glands. Your brain also releases adrenal glands when you have a goal. For example, when business owners are trying to make money or when athletes are trying to compete, they release adrenal glands. When you are calm, your brain releases serotonin during the daytime and melatonin during the night time. Emotions are mental feelings you experience in response to these biochemical reactions in the brain.

Although emotions come from biochemical reactions, they are still a whole lot more. Emotions are like the children of chemical reactions in the brain. Emotions are born from chemical reactions in the brain, but they have a life of their own. Also, simply controlling the brain's chemical reactions is not enough to cause happiness or sadness. You can give people drugs like morphine, and temporarily they may be happy, but in the long run, it will damage them. Thoughts and life experiences have a much more powerful affect on the brain. Doing activities that you enjoy and forming relationships with people you care about are the best ways to become happy. Poverty, physical abuse, and lack of control are things that cause unhappiness. Most mental patients have biochemical imbalances in their brain that lead to their conditions, but their life experiences cause those biochemical imbalances. Depression is caused by low serotonin levels in the brain, but low serotonin levels in the brain are caused by negative thoughts, abusive spouses and parents, or other life experiences.

Mindless Brain

We have so many different thoughts traveling throughout our brain, but is there anything that unites these thoughts? Is there a "mind" that is distinct from the brain? Mind is a convenient term to refer to our thoughts as a single unit, but in reality, there is no mind. We just have a brain that has thoughts. We are able to control our thoughts, but these thoughts still arise from and travel in our brain. If we do not have a brain, we do not have thoughts, we do not experience emotions, and we are not conscious. Although other living creatures may experience consciousness, in human and other animals, consciousness is only possible with a brain. When we die, we are no longer conscious, and we do not have thoughts or emotions. Rocks and other nonliving objects probably do not experience these ever.

Now what in the brain causes the brain to interpret something as negative or positive? I don't know the answer to that, and I won't even try to answer that. I am grateful that I am conscious and thus able to experience positive things. I am glad that I have friends and family that I care for. I am happy that I can do activities that I enjoy. Although I also experience unhappiness at times, my happy experiences more than make up for it. Unfortunately, many people around the world do not have as lucky of a life as I do. Millions of poor people around the world experience poverty, oppression, hunger, and other problems. As global citizens, we can donate to charity organizations or volunteer our time to help change their lives, which will help them experience a happier life.

Computers and Brains

If consciousness arises from the right combination of molecules to form nerves, brain chemicals, and other things; can humans create a computer or robot with human intelligence? Well, it may be possible with the right combination of software and hardware. That is, if humans design an electronic device using the right chips, right wires, right outer layer, and right software, they may be able to turn this electronic device into a conscious, living creature. Of course, not only do the software and hardware have to be right, but the conditions have to be right. For example, the first living creatures arose from a combination of ammonia, nitrogen, carbon dioxide, oxygen, and nucleic aids. This doesn't mean that any time you mix these molecules, you get a living creature. It just means that the proper combination of chemicals can possibly create life. Of course, this combination also has to have the right weather and other conditions. We have no record of life arising from nonliving matter. Why did life arise 3.5 billion years ago from nonliving matter but not now? Well, the temperature, atmosphere, and geography were completely different back then. Also, in our time, molecules might be "trying" to combine and form a simple living creature, but the movement of animals and other life stop that from happening. For example, if you were making a sand castle, and somebody kicked your sand castle every time you were about to finish, you will never have a sand castle. If there was nobody else around, you just might finish that sand castle. Maybe humans and other living creatures now are preventing matter from becoming life through our actions, whatever those actions may be.

Earth Values

All morals involve action of some sort. Killing is immoral because it takes away the life of somebody. Life is a physical property. Also, this living creature who is killed has family members and friends. Family is a biological issue, and biology is physical. Stealing is also physical. It involves movement to steal, and it involves taking a physical object.

You can also steal information, but information is still written down in a written language or computer code. This information is recorded on paper or stored, saved on a computer, stored in an internet server, or some other physical object. Rape is physical because it involves an action with a body. Even thoughts require a brain. So although rape is immoral because it involves a lack of consent, consent requires a brain.

In addition to immoral actions, there are positive values that are physical. Friendship itself may not be directly physical, but it involves people with physical bodies who meet each other to talk or to do activities. Communication involves sound or motion. Activities also involve motion.

If I were to say that it is immoral to kill air, that would make no sense. It also does not make sense to say that it is wrong to rape water. It is possible to pollute water and air, and this damages the health of humans and other animals who breathe air and drink water. However, it is impossible to kill air, so it would make no sense to say "killing air is immoral." It is possible to say that polluting air is immoral, but again, this is based on the physical reaction that air pollution causes. There is no abstract or spiritual basis against polluting air. So rather than having some abstract law to govern morals, all morals are based on the physical consequences of an action. Even intention, which doesn't appear physical, requires a brain.

So basically, you can some up morality with the Hippocratic oath...do no harm. Of course, morality is more than just avoiding things that harm others. It also includes doing things that spread happiness. You can argue that happiness is an abstract idea, but it is actually very physical. You need a brain to experience happiness. Happiness involves biochemical reactions with brain chemicals such as serotonin, adrenaline, dopamine, and many others. Happiness is something that you can "feel." Maybe not in the same sense as touching an object, but it is still a feeling. To be happy, you need friends, family, pets, etc. In other words...developing relationships with living creatures rather than abstract ideas gives happiness. You also experience happiness through hobbies, career, and other activities. Meditation and sleep can also give happiness.

You might think that a physical basis for morality is meaningless. Maybe it seems more meaningful to have an abstract, invisible force governing morals. I say the opposite is true. Morality based on abstract ideas is meaningless because it does not involve action. Values become much more meaningful when they are based on actions and living creatures that we can see, hear, and touch. We cannot play basketball with "a higher power." We cannot do other fun activities with it. We cannot help it when it is in need. A higher power doesn't help us when we are in need. People help each other when in need. Although some say that this higher power inspires people to help each other, I see no reason to include it. Why not be grateful to people for helping each? What reason do we need to add some "higher power" behind it? After all, even if a higher power exists, it needs something to be higher than. Without people, there can be no higher power.

Sources Cited

Adam M. Gadomski, ENEA, Italy; Jan M. Zytkow; (1995). "ABSTRACT INTELLIGENT AGENTS: PARADIGMS, FOUNDATIONS AND CONCEPTUALIZATION PROBLEMS." Reflections after The First International Round-Table on Abstract Intelligent Agent. (AIA93) Wichita State University, USA " Abstract Intelligent Agent, 2". Printed by ENEA, Rome, ISSN/1120-558X. http://erg4146.casaccia.enea.it/wwwerg26701/gad-zyt.htm

Professor Keith M Kendrick. "The Neurobiology of Social Bonds." (2007). The Babraham Institute Cambridge. British Society for Neuroendocrinology. http://www.neuroendo.org.uk/downloads/briefing_22.pdf

Arias-Carrión O, Pöppel E. (2007). "Dopamine, Learning, and Reward-Seeking Behavior." ACTA Neurobiology Experimentalis. http://www.ane.pl/pdf/6738.pdf

Stanley L. Miller. (May 1953). "Production of Amino Acids Under Possible Primitive Earth Conditions." Science. 117: 528. http://www.issol.org/miller/miller1953.pdf

Douglas Fox. (March 28, 2007). "Primordial Soup's On: Scientists Repeat Evolution's Most Famous Experiment" Scientific American. http://www.sciam.com/article.cfm?id=primordial-soup-urey-miller-evolution-experiment-repeated

Free Will Vs. Cause and Effect

Dynamic Universe

While Newtonian physics suggest a predictable and mechanical universe, quantum physics shows that the location and velocity of sub-atomic particles cannot both be predicted at the same time. We can only predict where it is at a given instant or the velocity is moving, but not both at the same time. Chaos theory shows that slight changes in the conditions of matter can cause huge changes in the end result. As the saying goes, a butterfly flapping its wings in Texas can cause an earthquake in China.

One Cause, Many Outcomes

Many people wonder what causes people to become evil and what causes us to do good. Many psychologists and neuroscientists debate whether nature or nurture has more control on a person's actions. What they ignore is that in addition to nature and nurture, people also can make an individual choice in response to nature and nurture.

Some people assume that because cause and effect exist, we have no free will. However, this is false. Although every event has a cause, each cause can have multiple possible outcomes. For example, if I punch you, you might punch me back. The fact that I punched you caused you to punch me back. However, you also have the option to not punch me. You might yell at me instead. Although it is unlikely, you also can respond in just about any other way. You could laugh at me, kiss me, hug me, or have any other weird reaction. If I punch you, and then you hug me immediately afterward, the fact that I punched you caused you to hug me. This doesn't mean you don't have free will. It just means my action of punching you can have multiple possible outcomes, and you chose one of them. Or hell, maybe you might kiss me and then punch me back. Either way you look at it, cause and effect are perfectly compatible with free will. Cause and effect and like a tree with multiple branches.

Biochemistry affects our decision-making. Hormones such as adrenaline and dopamine get us excited. When we are excited, we usually behave differently than when we are calm or sad. However, just because hormones in our brain affect our behavior does not mean that they dictate our behavior. It is possible to be depressed and still take action take action rather than sit down and complain. Likewise, it is possible to be excited and be lazy rather than take action. Although genes, biochemistry, and life experiences shape who we are, how we react to those circumstances determines who we become. Circumstances may limit us, but we don't know what those limits are. There are many possible outcomes despite such limitations. Being poor with low serotonin levels may lead somebody to become a criminal, but it may also lead that person to be passive. In other cases, this same person may work so hard and become a rags to riches story.

Biology of Evil

Damage to the brain and irregular amounts of brain chemicals do affect a person's choices in life. Problems in the brain alone do not cause people to become evil. Most evil people come from a very harsh upbringing. This isn't to justify evil behavior, but it does show that environment has more to do with behavior than biology. In fact, environment often affects biology. If you look at most people with neurological problems, most of them come from a harsh background of poverty and violence. Abuse can cause low serotonin levels and low levels of dopamine. The neo-cortex of the brain is responsible for decision-making, so abuse may cause damage to that area. Insufficient blood supply to the brain is also linked with evil people. However, a lifetime of doing evil may cause the insufficient blood supply ratherthan insufficient blood supply causing evil behavior. Just as mental stress can cause high blood pressure, anger can cause insufficient blood supply to the frontal lobe or the limbic system, which processes emotions.

Of course, regardless of upbringing or biology, most evil people still make choices. Most poor people or mentally handicapped people do not become evil. Many criminals even have normal brains and come from stable, middle-class families. Jeffry Dahmer is an example of somebody who psychologists say is mentally normal, but he still chose to take actions that are evil.

Evil Throughout History

Many of us take for granted that there are laws against violence, rape, theft, etc. For most of human history, there were no such laws. Tribes killed each other for land and food. They even raped women from other tribes to spread their genes. There was no consensus that such acts are immoral. Killing was considered wrong only if it was done to your tribe; killing was accepted when done to the other tribe. Raping and stealing from members of other tribes was also considered acceptable. You can argue that this behavior is hard-wired into our brains. However, in addition to tribal warfare, many tribes traded with each other and even became friends with each other. Sometimes tribes merged to form larger tribes. Tribes had a choice between warfare and cooperation. Sometimes they chose warfare, and in other cases, they chose cooperation. In fact, they eventually made the choice to leave tribal systems and become civilizations.

Legal systems started with civilization. Ancient Egypt had a law code written on tablets at about 3000 B.C. Hammurabi started a law code in 1760 B.C. These law codes were not perfect, but they extended morality outside of tribes and spread them throughout cities. These civilizations still practiced slavery, and they still pillaged other cities. However, they were still a big improvement over the tribal morality that came before them. Also, over time, civilizations improved their moral standards by abolishing slavery, giving rights to women and racial minorities, etc.

The United States of America, which we honor as the land of freedom, actually restricted rights for most of its people during most of American history. Freedom was only given to white, Anglo-Saxon, Protestant, land-owning males. We often honor America's founding fathers such as Thomas Jefferson, but some of them owned slaves and murdered Native Americans. Certainly, this should be viewed as evil.

I doubt Thomas Jefferson had abnormal brain function. His biology did not cause him to commit these horrible crimes. His thirst for wealth and desire for American "democracy" motivated him to kill innocent Native Americans and deny freedom to other innocent African Americans. His greed caused him to act this way, but he chose to act on his greed. He could have chosen not to act on greed.

Karma

Many people believe in the law of karma. They believe people get punished for their evil deeds and rewarded for good deeds. In many cases, this can be true, but this is often not the case.

Saddam Hussein got punished for his crimes, but the people he tortured suffered far more than he did. So in this case, the evil person suffered less than the good people. Hitler committed suicide when the Soviet Union invaded Germany, but this is nothing compared to the suffering he caused millions of innocent people. Although Hitler and Saddam Hussein suffered somewhat for their crimes, not everybody does. The founding fathers of America were not punished for owning slaves and killing Native Americans.

So there really is no law of karma. Sometimes people get punished for wrong-doing, but that is only when other people step in to punish them. People get rewarded for doing good only when other people step in to give the reward.

Also, good and evil are not always easy to identify. For example, most people would honor the founder of McDonald's for starting the first major franchise. Ray Kroc was not the founder, but he turned McDonald's into a major corporation and franchise. He gave thousands of people the opportunity to own a McDonald's restaurant through franchising. So how can he be evil? Well, think of all the animal suffering caused by making burgers. Also, think of all the people that suffered heart disease and even heart attacks from eating all those McDonald's burgers. Now does that mean Ray Kroc is evil?

Well, maybe Ray Kroc is just a normal person who is trying to make money, and the best way he knew was selling meat products. We all need money to survive. Unfortunately selling meat products might be the easiest way for Ray Kroc to make money. I doubt that Ray Kroc purposely chose to sell burgers because he enjoys seeing animals killed. Also, burgers are still food, and unfortunately, humans need to take either the life of plants or the life of animals to survive. Modern day American plants are poor sources of vitamin B12, so we either need multi-vitamins or animal products to get vitamin B12. So you could argue that Ray Kroc is cashing in on something we need for survival. Sure, he could have started selling multi-vitamins, but he probably wouldn't make a lot of money doing that because that is not his area of expertise.

You could argue that oil companies are evil because they cause so much pollution and because they get petroleum from Middle Eastern countries that support terrorism. However, they do that deliberately. Oil happened to be the cheapest and most energy dense fuel source for automobiles. In addition to causing harm, it created a lot of good. Cars allow us to get to work more quickly, which makes us more productive. Ambulances may not have been as quick without oil. We are able to travel to different countries to do trade and learn about different cultures because of oil. It is not the fault of oil companies for the fact that oil causes pollution. It is also not their fault that Saudi Arabia and other Middle Easter countries are the biggest suppliers of oil. We definitely should move toward alternative fuel sources, but despite the suffering caused by oil, you would have to be careful before calling oil companies evil. After all, we buy gasoline for our cars, so we are just as responsible for pollution and funding terrorism as they are.

Instead of thinking about punishment and reward, I prefer to think of ways to reduce suffering and improve happiness.

Stopping Evil

We cannot for sure prevent people from becoming evil, but we can change the environment in which we live. This can reduce the risk of people that become evil. Most people that commit evil actions come from harsh backgrounds of poverty and abuse. Although we cannot intervene in all families to prevent abuse, we can reduce poverty by supporting charity organizations such as CARE. Organizations like CARE improve the economy of third world countries. The website for

CARE is www.care.org. In the US, we can support organizations such as Boys & Girls Club and After School All-Stars. These organizations help keep young people from underprivileged backgrounds off of the streets and out of gangs. We can either donate to them or directly volunteer for them.

Despite all the evil in this world, FBI and other statistics show that violent and other crimes are dropping. Even though we see acts of terrorism and governments killing their own people, the overall trend in this world is that people are becoming more connected. Although Bhutan is trying to eliminate it's Nepalese population, it is a much better nation than before. It is a Buddhist theocracy with almost no freedom, and now it is trying to become a constitutional democracy. It still is not a free nation, but it never was.

Terrorists from the Middle East and Central Asia are killing thousands of innocent people, but before modern times, governments from these countries killed millions of innocent people simply because they were not Muslim. Instead of killing their own people, they invaded other countries to spread Islam by force. So overall, morality in the Middle East has improved. In some Muslim countries, women's rights are greatly improving. Turkey, Indonesia, and Malaysia are examples of moderate Muslim nations that also have better human rights records. During World War 1, Turkey killed over a million innocent Aremenians and millions of others in Greece and elsewhere. It was a Muslim theocracy that spread Islam by force. Now, Turkey honours separation of church and state. Indonesia's governments in the past killed hundreds of thousand innocent people from Timor. The past ruler Suharto killed over a million Chinese living in Indonesia. Now, Indonesia's human rights record has greatly improved.

In Africa, Latin America, and Asia; human rights are also improving. Living standards are improving. Women are getting careers. These changes show that although situations can movitate us to commit evil acts, over time, we can make the choice to do good instead of evil.

Sources Cited:

"Functional Families, Dysfunctional Brains." (Apr. 10, 1998). Science Daily.
http://www.sciencedaily.com/releases/1998/04/980410101830.htm

Scott O. Lilienfeld and Hal Arkowitz (2007). "What Psychopath Means: It is not quite what you may think." Scientific American.
http://www.sciam.com/article.cfm?id=what-psychopath-means&page=2

"Psychopath Psychologist Adds Scientific Insight To Loaded Label." (July 5 2006). Medical News Today.
http://www.medicalnewstoday.com/articles/46444.php

"Crime in the United States 2004." Federal Bureau of Investigation. Murder. Updated 2/17/2006.
http://www.fbi.gov/ucr/cius_04/offenses_reported/violent_crime/murder.html

"Living on the Edge of Chaos." Peter Gleeson and Dr Eddy Kloprogge, January 2007 .
http://www.mind-gliding.co.uk/articles/lec.htm

Scott O. Lilienfeld and Hal Arkowitz. "What Psychopath Means."
http://www.sciam.com/article.cfm?id=what-psychopath-means

"What is Chaos Theory?"
http://iit.ches.ua.edu/systems/chaos.html

The Gates of Time

What is Time?

Time is a concept that puzzles scientists and philosophers. Most societies in the world have some way of measuring or keeping tracking of time. Although hourly time isn't universal, most societies have a calendar that measures time by the sun or moon. One year is the time it takes for the Earth to revolve around the sun in the solar calendar. For the lunar calendar, a year is the time it takes the moon to revolve around the sun.

While time seems abstract, modern physics suggests that time is physical. This may be hard to believe, but when you think about it, we all "feel" time. That is, we can sense the difference between 5 hours and 2 minutes. Of course, our sensation of time is not perfect. It can be difficult to tell the difference between 45 minutes and 40 minutes or 13 hours and 12 hours. Nonetheless, we still have some sense of what time feels like.

Time Travel

Movies and books have been written about time travel. However, nobody has ever traveled through time in real life. Most scientists suggest that time it is possible to slow down time, but this only occurs when traveling at the speed of light.

Some scientists suggest that we can go back in time to observe the past but cannot change it. Whatever science says about time, we may never really know if time travel is possible, but it is a fun topic to discuss. Even if we can't travel through time, measuring time is very useful for our lives. We plan our careers, social life, and other things around time. Right now, we measure time in a system of 60 seconds in a minute, 60 minutes in an hour, 24 hours in a day, 7 days in a week, and

365 days in a year. However, there are alternative systems of time that some people advocate.

Metric Time

Most of the world measures distance, volume, length, mass, and other measurements in units of 10. While Americans measure distance in miles and inches, the rest of the world uses kilometers and centimeters. This system that uses units of 10 is called the metric system. If I asked you how many inches are in a mile, it would take you a long time. There are 12 inches in a foot and 5,280 feet in a mile. Although you can use a calculator to calculate it, it would takes some time to do it on paper, and it is nearly impossible to do it in your head. Now if I asked you how many centimeters are in a kilometer, you can calculate easily. There are 100 centimeters in a meter and 1000 meters in a kilometer. Just add the zeroes to get 100,000 centimeters in a kilometer. Mass involves using milligrams, grams, and kilograms. You can change from one unit to the other easily by multiplying or diving by 10, 100, 1000, etc.

While most of the world uses the much simpler metric system for most things, they follow Americans in using much more difficult way of calculating time. America did not invent the system of using 60 seconds in a minute, 60 minutes in an hour, and 24 hours in a day. This came from Mesopotamia. The number 12, for some reason, was considered a holy number. This eventually influenced Christianity; Jesus had 12 disciples. In the story of King Arthur, the Knights of the Round sat in a table of 12. We Although we currently have a 24 hour day, this is divided into two cycles of 12 hours. European colonialism and American imperialism has influenced the rest of the world to adopt this system of measuring time.

Instead of units of 10 and 100, the world measures times in units of 60 and 24. There are 60 seconds in a minute, 60 minutes in an hour, and 24 hours in a day. Wouldn't it be simpler if they had 100 seconds in a minute, 100 minutes in an hour, and 10 hours in a day?

There are actually alternative systems of time that some people use, especially in the information technology industry. However, they use different units. Instead of dividing a day into 24 hours, they divide a day into 10 cycles. Each cycle is divided into 100 moments, which are similar to minutes. Moments are further divided into ticks, which are an alternative unit for seconds. Here is a comparison of how these metric units for time compare to the units we use today.

1 tick=0.86 seconds
1 moment=1.44 minutes
1 cycle-2.4 hours

Calendar

The original Julian calendar had 10 months. Later, July was added in honor of Julius Caesar while August was added after the death of his son Caesar Augustus. We could go back to the Julian Calendar and use the original 10 months. However, during the transition from the old calendar to the metric, it would confuse a lot of people when they say "we are meeting January 10." So it is best to have a whole new set of months.

To have a metric calendar, we need to have a multiple of 10 for the number of days for both the months and the years. We could have a 100 day year, but that would mean each month has only 10 days. I recommend having 100 days per month so that a year is 1000 days.

For the names of the days, there are two different calendars that catch people's attention. Below are the calendars and the names of the days.

Annus Novus Decimal Calendar

1) Primus
2) Secundus
3) Tertius
4) Quartarius
5) Quintus
6) Sextarius
7) Septimus
8) Octavus
9) Nonus
10) Decimus

New Digital Standard Calendar

1) 0 = Nuller
2) 1 = Prier
3) 2 = Secter
4) 3 = Trier
5) 4 = Quattrer
6) 5 = Penter
7) 6 = Sexter
8) 7 = Septer
9) 8 = Octer
10) 9 = None

Each metric month would be separated into 10 metric weeks. Each metric week would have 10 days instead of 7. It would be too confusing if we used the 7 days we have now and then added 3 days, so it is better just to have 10 entirely new days. Here are some examples used during the French Republican Calendar (a period in the 1700s when the French expirmented with metric time).

1) Primidi
2) Duodi
3) Tridi
4) Quartidi

5) Quintidi
6) Sextidi
7) Septidi
8) Octodi
9) Nonidi
10) Decadi

Now this would be an example of a calendar:

Primus 2010

Primi-di	Duo-di	Tridi	Quartidi	Quintidi	Sexti-di	Septi-di	Octodi	Nonidi	Decadi
1	2	3	4	5	6	7	8	9	10
11	12	13	14	15	16	17	18	19	20
21	22	23	24	25	26	27	28	29	30
31	32	33	34	35	36	37	38	39	40
41	42	43	44	45	46	47	48	49	50
51	52	53	54	55	56	57	58	59	60
61	62	63	64	65	66	67	68	69	70
71	72	73	74	75	76	77	78	79	80
81	82	83	84	85	86	87	88	89	90
91	92	93	94	95	96	97	98	99	100

There are also other examples of metric calendars.

New Digital Standar Calendar

1) 0 = Yourday
2) 1 = Myday
3) 2 = Momday
4) 3 = Dadday
5) 4 = Poorday
6) 5 = Giveday
7) 6 = Getday

8) 7 = Workday
9) 8 = Loveday
10) 9 = Restday

Here is a metric week proposal from the site "A Guide to Metric Time."

1) Zeroday (D0)
2) Oneday (D1)
3) Twoday (D2)
4) Threeday (D3)
5) Fourday (D4)
6) Fiveday (D5)
7) Sixday (D6)
8) Sevenday (D7)
9) Eightday (D8)
10) Nineday (D9)

I am not sure if we will ever use metric time. It will be a very hard transition since we are so used to using our current system of measuring time. However, who knows if we will eventually change this system? We have changed things in the past, and wel will continue to change things that we are used to in favor of things that are more practical. Maybe a new way of measuring time is one of those changes. Only time will tell.

Sources Cited

Hawking, Stephen. "The Beginning of Time". University of Cambridge. Retrieved on January 10,2008.
http://www.hawking.org.uk/lectures/bot.html

"RECYCLED UNIVERSE THEORY COULD SOLVE COSMIC MYSTERY." (MAY 8, 2006).
http://www.space.com/scienceastronomy/060508_mm_cyclic_universe.html

"W HAT HAPPENED BEFORE THE BIG BANG". RETRIEVED ON JULY 3, 2007.
http://www.science.psu.edu/alert/Bojowald6-2007.htm

Rich Groleau. "Think Like Einstein."
http://www.pbs.org/wgbh/nova/time/think.html

Clifford Pickover. "Traveling Through Time."
http://www.pbs.org/wgbh/nova/time/through.html

"Decimal Time-Calendars"
http://www.decimaltime.hynes.net/calendar.html#ndsc

"A Guide to Metric Time."
http://zapatopi.net/metrictime/week.html

Super Hero Logic

Superheroes such as Superman and Batman are very popular in the US and other countries. As powerful as superheroes are physically, their greatest strength may be their ability to go beyond the rules of logic. Let's start with Superman. Why does he wear underwear over his uniform? Would it make him any less powerful if he wore it under (after all, it is called UNDERwear, not OVERwear)? Maybe if he wore it under, he would look naked. Well, maybe they should give him a less revealing uniform. Also, does he always wear the same exact outfit, or does he have an entire wardrobe of the same uniform? Does he put his uniform in the laundry, or do superheroes have their own way to clean clothes? Hell, maybe when superheroes have a hidden superpower that they never tell us about. Maybe they live off their own cleaning detergent. I wonder which part of their body it comes from. hmm...maybe superheroes take a pee, the stuff that comes out is a cleaning solution rather than nasty stuff. Maybe Superman cleans his clothes by pissing on them. I wonder if his shit is also a cleaning solution.

As most people know, Clark Kent is Superman's secret identity. Can somebody please explain to me why superheroes need a secret identity? Are they afraid nobody will hire them if they give out their real identities? I doubt it would make much difference to the Daily Planet if Superman applied for the job using his real name Kal-El. He doesn't have to mention that he has super strength or mention that he was born on Krypton. Of course, it is unlikely that job opportunity has anything to do with why Superman disguises his identity. I think the real reason is that it would be dangerous if the wrong people learn about his powers. Again, can somebody please explain why Superman is so afraid of villains knowing he has super powers. How could knowing that he is super powerful be of any advantage to them? I would think that it would scare them away from crime if they knew how powerful he is. Is Superman afraid that they will somehow be able to use his powers for evil? Well, I don't see the logic behind it. As long as they are unable to control his mind, they can't use his powers. In fact, being so powerful, it would actually be very hard for criminals to manipulate Superman. Also, these criminals find out about his super powers as soon as he attacks them.

Speaking of Superman's secret identity, how is it that nobody could figure out that Superman and Clark Kent are the same people? Is it because Superman has tight suit and underwear while Clark wears a tuxedo? Well, when I change my clothes, nobody seems to have trouble knowing that I am the same person. People should be able to figure out that Clark Kent and Superman at least related. Maybe Superman and Clark Kent are twin brothers. They look too much alike for people not to notice some relation. Maybe Superman's uniform has the superpower of deflecting people's recognition skills. Maybe his uniform also can damage people's memory. In Superman 2, Louis realizes that Clark is Superman when fire touches Clark's hand, but it has no effect. She responds with the words "You really are Superman." However, somehow she manages to forget that in Superman 3 and Superman 4. How can anybody forget something like that? Nobody has a perfect memory, but I think that would be a pretty hard thing to forget that your boyfriend can lift an entire building, is able to fly, and is immune to pain. Although it is nice that Superman keeps saving people, he should also try teaching people how to defend themselves. If he is so powerful, he must be able to share his powers. Superman could leave his job on the Daily Planet and be a full-time martial arts instructor to teach people how to have super powers like him. Now that could really make him money.

Where does Superman get his super powers from? Is it purely genetic, or does he follow a very strict exercise and dietary program? I would love to see what kind of workouts Superman does and what kind of food he eats. Somebody could make a lot of money selling "The Superman Diet." I don't think that his powers could have come only from his good genes. After all, his entire planet became extinct. They couldn't all be super powerful, can they? I guess the creator of Superman hasn't heard of the phrase "Survival of the Fittest." Last time I checked, the strongest and smartest live while everybody else dies out.

Now lets talk about Clark Kent and his work at the Daily Planet. Clark works as a news reporter. Every now and then, something bad happens, so Clark leaves his job and turns into Superman. I would love to know how Clark manages to avoid getting fired for skipping work so often. Does he claim that he is taking a bathroom break? Well, he must have some serious biological problems if it takes that long to use the bathroom. Also, Clark has a relationship with Louis Lane, who also works at the Daily Planet. Isn't there some kind of policy against co-workers dating, or did they somehow have trouble figuring out the nature of Louis and Clark's relationship? Hell, maybe they are open-minded and decided that there is no real reason to fire employees just because they are boning each other.

Although Superman is very powerful, he seems to be extremely allergic to kryptonite. How could he be allergic to the very rock that came from his home planet? In fact, the nature of his planet makes me wonder a few things. Superman's father Jar-El sent Superman to Earth to save him from the destruction of Krypton. In order to send him to Earth without crashing into something, Jar-El had to shoot him into space with the perfect amount of gravitational force and velocity. It had to take a lot of time to learn this skill. In the time it took to learn how to toy with the laws of physics to send his son off to Earth, he could have figured out how to save his planet or how to send his whole planet to Earth. In fact, what exactly is the reason why Krypton was under siege? How can a race of super humans become extinct while a planet of normal humans provide a safe haven for the last surviving superhuman? Also, how is it that the people of Krypton know English? I know the British colonized a large part of the world, but I do not recall the British Empire being an intergalactic federation? Maybe my knowledge of history is off, but I don't recall the British colonizing Krypton.

The enemies of superheroes never seize to amaze me. How do they keep returning back from the "dead?" Do they somehow get emergency surgery right on the spot after the superhero kills them? If so, how do these superheroes fail to notice until the sequel comes out a few years later?

A lot of people don't know this, but Kal-El is Hebrew for "vessel of God." El is short for Elohim, which is Hebrew for God. Is Superman

Jewish? While Superman's name is Kal-El, his father's name is Jar-El. I don't know what Jar-El means, but I have an interesting theory. If Superman is a "vessel of God," does that make Jar-El God himeself? Hmmm...maybe I should stop thinking so much. It is making my brain hurt. Maybe all this is too much for a mere mortal like me to think about.

A Humorous Twist to Life's Mysteries

Philosophy, science, and religion discuss many of life's mysteries such as the origin of the universe, where we came from, and other metaphysical ideas. I discuss such issues in this book, but I would also like to discuss many mysteries that you never hear about. Because humor is a very important part of health, I plan to emphasize the humorous mysteries in this chapter rather than the deep, philosophical ones that you usually hear about.

Many people have chapped lips. I sure do. We use Vaseline, chap stick, lip balm, and other remedies to treat chapped lips. It's very convenient living in 21st century American and having access to instant lip relief whether you go to the grocery store, pharmacy, gas station, or other place. I don't know how I can live if I didn't have this easy access. I am curious what people did before they had these modern lip treatments. I'm sure that chapped lips didn't start in the 20th century. My guess is that they used some sort of oil. Some people probably used butter. However, before people had auto-mobiles, they had to travel places by foot. Most people were farmers barely making a living, so they had to travel several miles to get water and other things. Wealthy people like kings traveled long distances for war or trade. Merchants also traveled long distances for trade. What did they do when their lips got chapped? Did the king have an official "lip oil" carrier travel with him? Maybe he told his cooks to save the oil from the meat so he could apply it on his lips.

Why does shit smell bad? It is basically the food we eat. Supposedly the bad smell comes from bacteria. Well, bacteria are all around us, so according to that logic, we should get a bad smell all day. I don't remember smelling bacteria.

As far as I know, everybody in this world farts. I also believe most people urinate and also give off solid waste from their backside. What happens when you have to go in the middle of war? I'm sure there are military camps where people go. When people are in war, there are obviously break periods for eating and other things. But what happens when you have to go in the middle of war? I mean REALLY have to go in the middle of war. Maybe you find a tree and start peeing, or you dig a ditch to get rid of wastes. But what happens when a soldier is coming after you while you are taking a dump? Do you quickly lift your pants up to attack back, or do you assume that you smell so bad that your enemy soldier will spare you to avoid coming near your horrible odor? Perhaps in that brief moment, your friends have time to attack the enemy. Maybe taking a dump makes you vulnerable to attack, but it probably also throws the enemy off for at least a brief moment. If you have to take a piss, just pee on your enemy. I don't care if he has a bazooka. In that brief moment when he is coming after you and sees you peeing (especially if you pee on him) or taking a dump, your buddies have time to attack the enemy. The enemy will be thinking "Why I am I looking at a half naked guy taking a dump?" So maybe that should be a common war tactic. Somebody needs to write another war strategy book: "Art of War 2: Biological Warfare." One chapter should be devoted to using bodily functions. Maybe they should create new weapons of mass destruction...shit bombs and urine beams. Imagine having UN weapons inspectors for those kinds of weapons. If they find those weapons, they just might die of bad odor before they can report these weapons.

Humans weren't always able to talk. When did they start, and how did they decide what words to use? In fact, how did they decide what symbols to use for written language?

When people sin, why don't they get immediate punishment? Imagine if every time you steal, your nose gets bigger. Every time you kill somebody, you get this rash all over your body, especially in private places. Every time you practice business fraud or cheat customers, your lips get swollen. Wouldn't that virtually eliminate crime and sin?

Epilogue

We hope you enjoyed this book; we especially hope you will use information from this book to improve your lives and make the world a better place. Although the different topics seemed scattered, they all shared the common goal of helping people think outside of the box. Rather than just talk about how things should change, we put effort to give information to people on how they can change whether it means changing our behavior, volunteering, donating to a charity, changing our diets, etc. Talk is cheap, and we didn't want to just preach how we think the world should function. We wanted to give information on how people can actually go about changing the world.

This book was also meant to entertain. Some of the chapters in the book were for pure humor. As we mention the health benefits of humor, we wanted this book to also provide humor. If you got new information and had a laugh, we achieved our goal.